CW01307644

© 2024 Playful & Active Mind Books. All rights reserved. No part of this book may be reproduced, distributed, or transmitted in any form or by any means, including photocopying, recording, or other electronic or mechanical methods, without the prior written permission of the publisher. Unauthorized sale or publication of this material is strictly prohibited. For permission requests, write to the publisher at the address below.
Playful & Active Mind Books
info@playfulandactivemindbooks.com

www.playfulandactivemindbooks.com

Scan the QR code to access **50 pages filled with affirmations, reflections, and recipes to support and guide you through every stage of your first period.** Discover how amazing you are!

Download the link you'll find inside and enjoy watching your kids spend hours entertained and learning. Take advantage of this exclusive offer!

Your opinion matters! On the last page, you'll find a link to leave your review. We'd love to hear your thoughts, and we'd be very grateful if you could share them with us.

Your strength and bravery are your superpowers. Never give up!

Hello, little *heroine*!

In every page of this story, beyond the illustrations and words, we want you to feel the power you carry inside. This story is made especially for you, to remind you that you are strong, brave, and capable of achieving anything you set your mind to. Every time you feel doubtful or insecure, remember that a star shines in your heart, lighting your way.

You have the power to change the world, to dream big, and to face any challenge with a smile. Never forget that you are amazing just as you are and that every step you take brings you closer to your dreams. Lift your head, show your courage, and move forward with confidence and joy!

The world is yours!

Index

Chapter 1: Val and Her World 7

Chapter 2: The Surgery and the Fear 25

Chapter 3: Inspiration and First Steps 47

Chapter 4: Overcoming and New Horizons 61

Chapter 1: Val and Her World

This is the story of Val, a 7-year-old girl with a smile so bright it could light up the darkest room. Even on the gloomiest days, she radiated warmth, spreading her light to everyone around her.

Val lived with her parents and her baby sister Lourdes in a bustling city where skyscrapers touched the sky and life never slowed down.

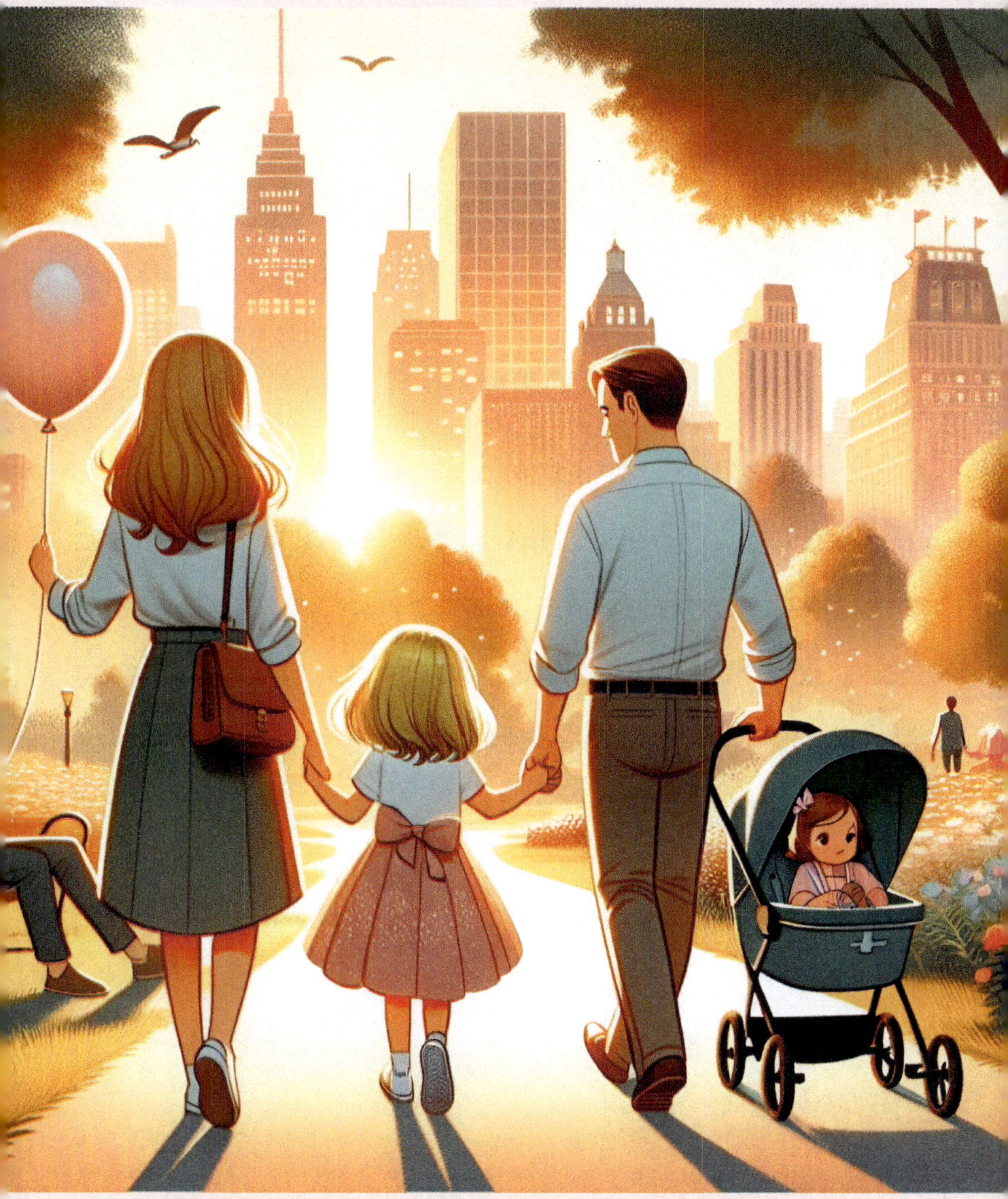

Val's home was always filled with joy, laughter, and an endless array of games.

In her room, decorated with stars and clouds on the walls, she taught her sister Lourdes new words and games, sharing her love for stories and adventures where heroines, armed with courage and wit, faced challenges, solved mysteries, and saved kingdoms from adversity.

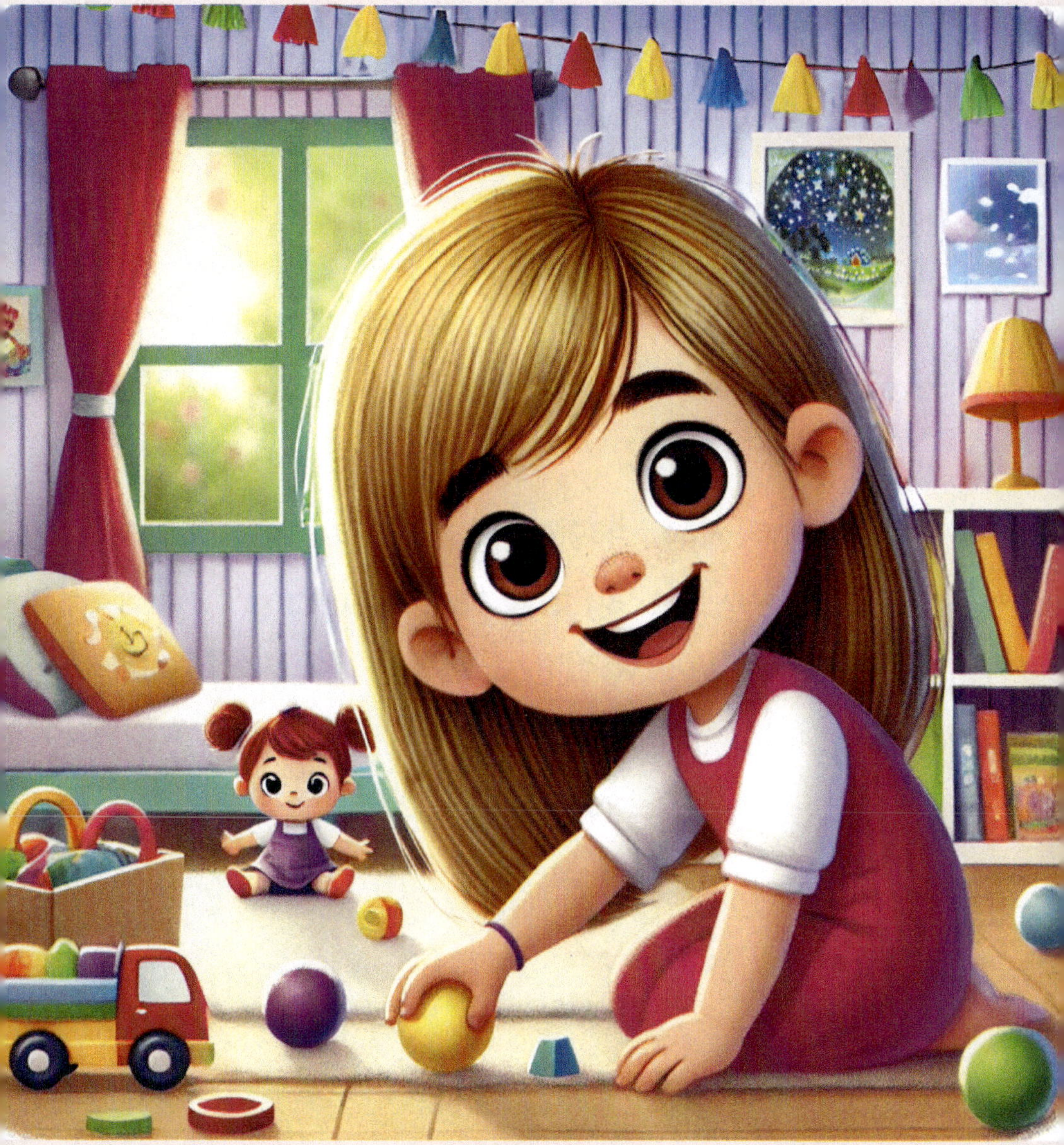

From a very young age, Val had learned to see the world through a different lens.

At birth, she was diagnosed with a developmental disorder in her left leg that caused it to grow slower than her right leg, resulting in her first steps being somewhat late and unsteady.

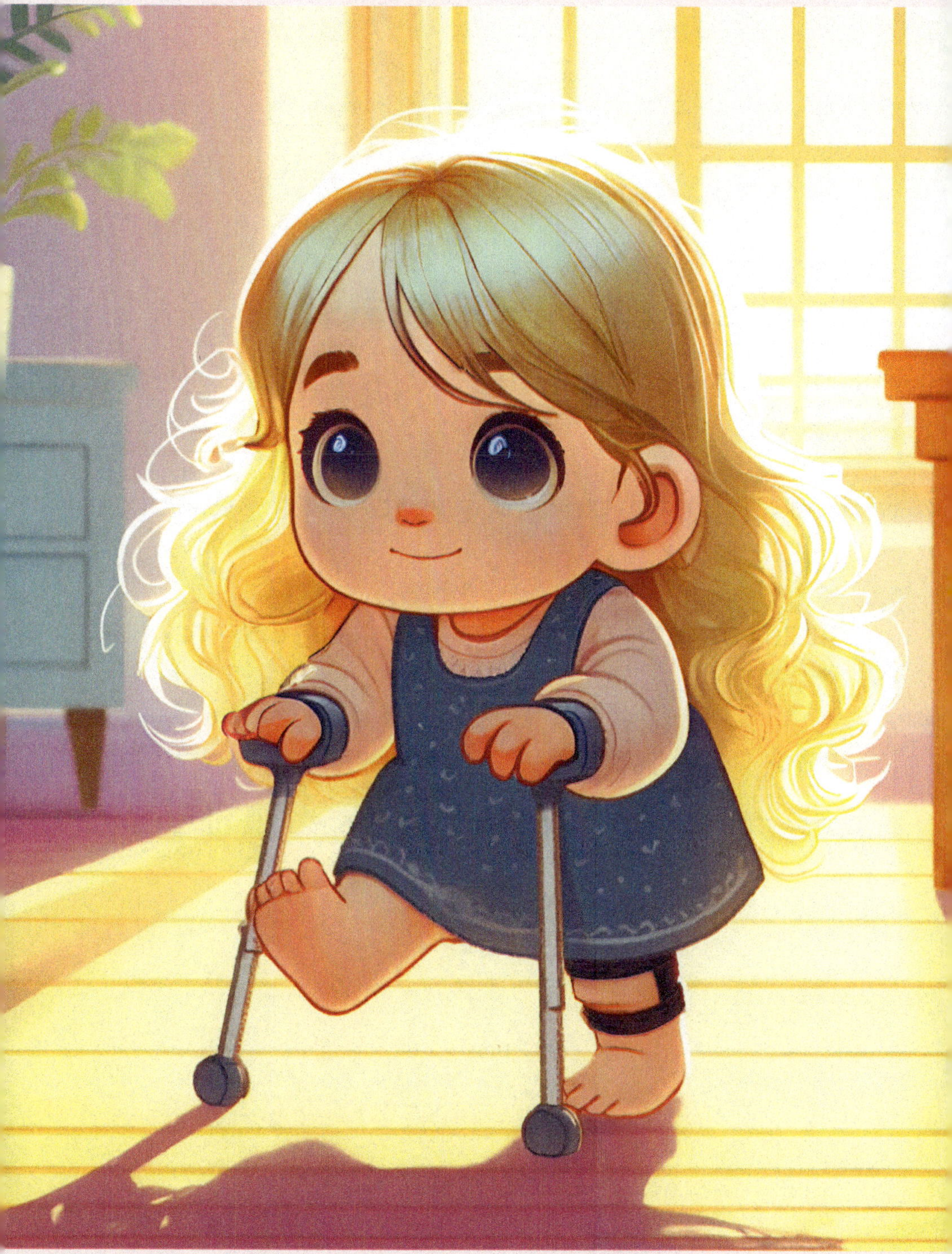

As she grew older, she needed to wear a lift in her shoe to help her walk, run, and play like the other kids.

Despite being a cheerful girl, loved by everyone who knew her for her energy, manners, and way of relating to others, not everything was easy for her.

There were moments, especially when playing with other children or at school, when she felt different.

15

Curious by nature, children often asked why she wore an orthopedic shoe with a lift.

Val always tried to respond with a shy smile, saying, "It's to help me walk and run better," although deep down she struggled to find the right words to explain her situation without feeling left out.

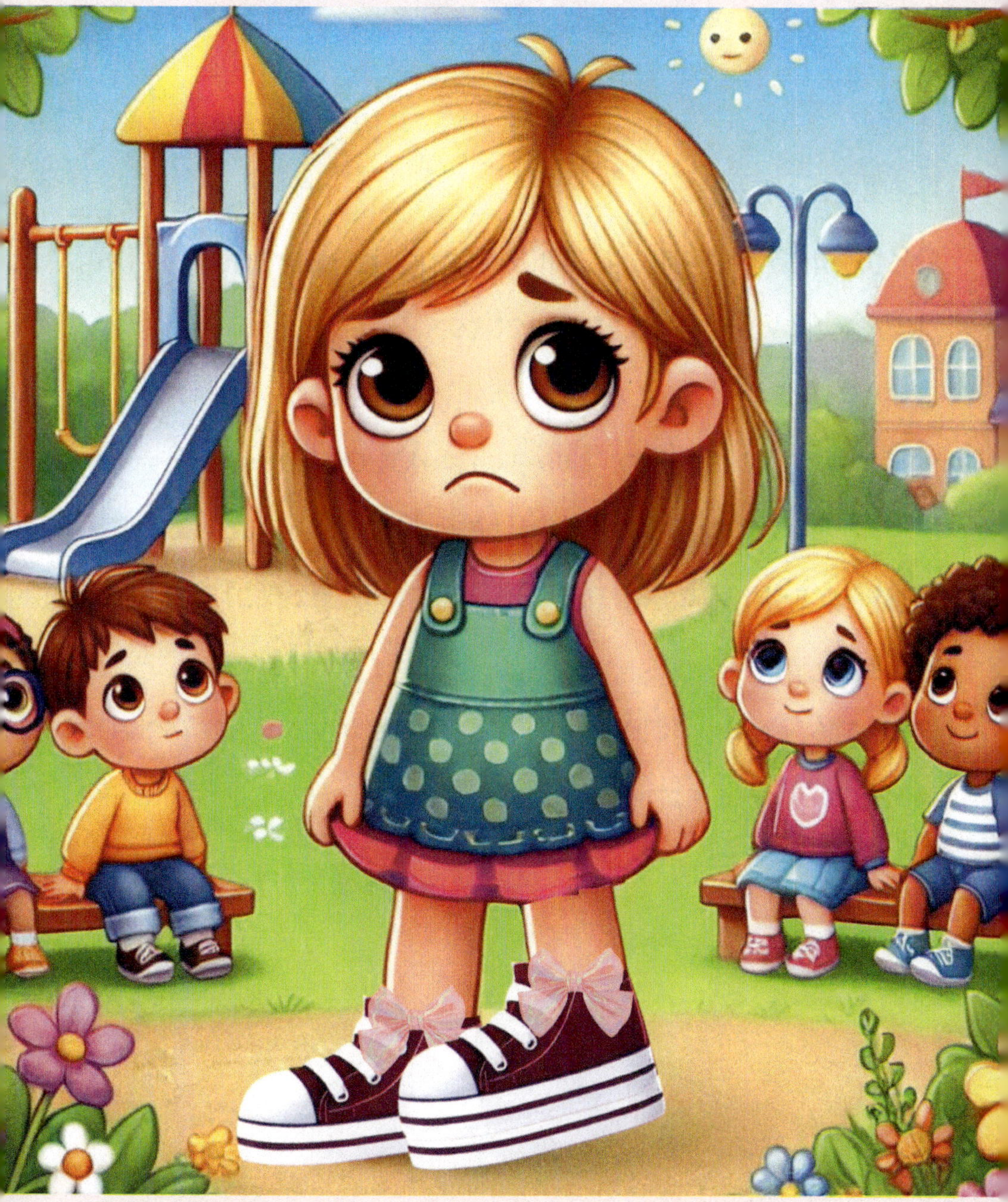

Val, who was very willing and determined, always looked for ways to stay active.

Her mom thought of swimming not only as a sport that could spark a passion in her daughter but also as a way to improve her mobility and feel free in the water.

So, she began going several times a week to practice this complete sport.

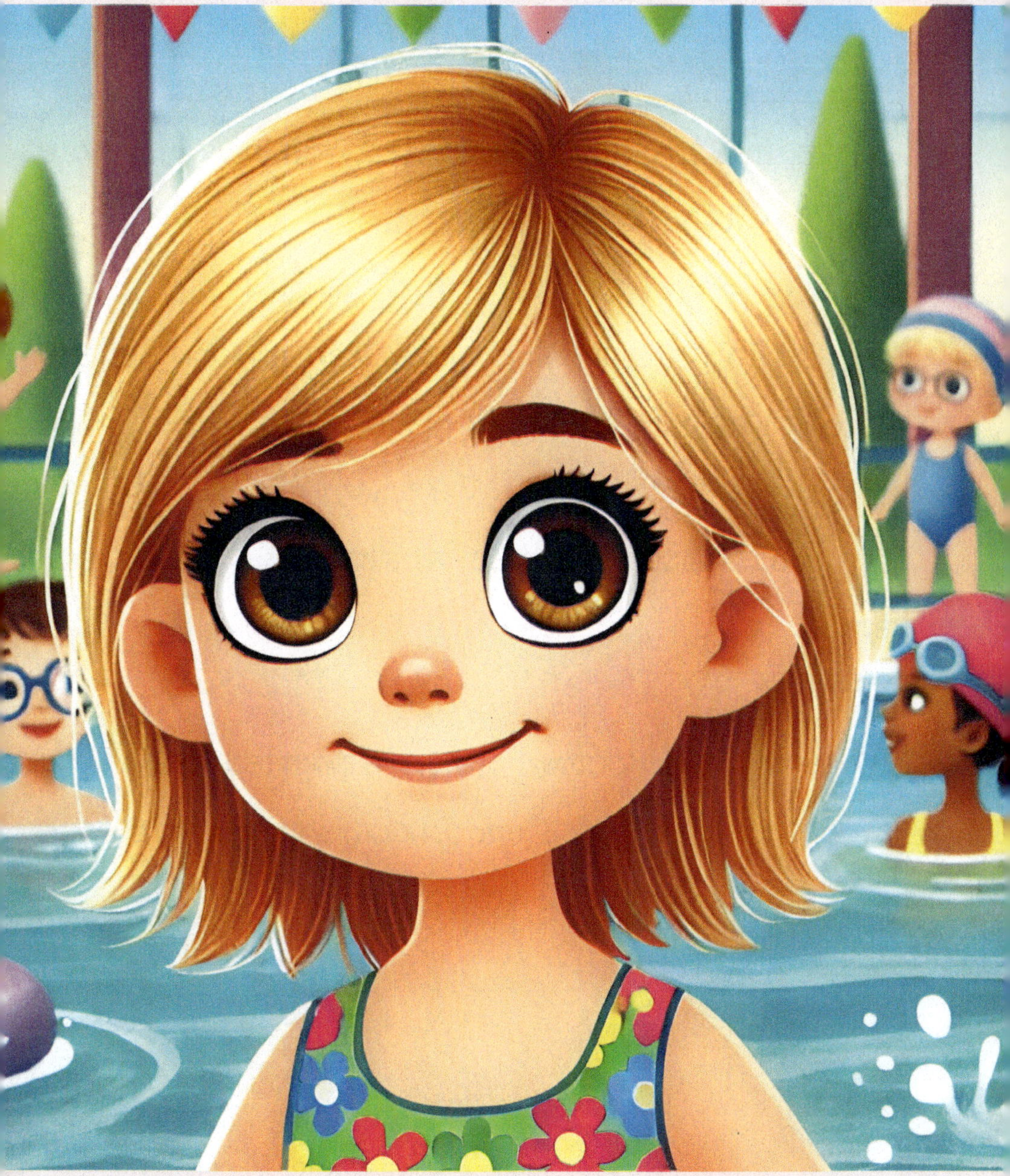

Despite the challenges she faced, she never let her condition define who she was.

Now she loved swimming more than anything in the world; it was her refuge, the place where she felt most like herself. In the water, Val wasn't the girl with the orthopedic shoe; she was a swimmer, strong and capable.

Her family and doctors always supported her, giving her positive messages and encouraging her to face her fears with courage.

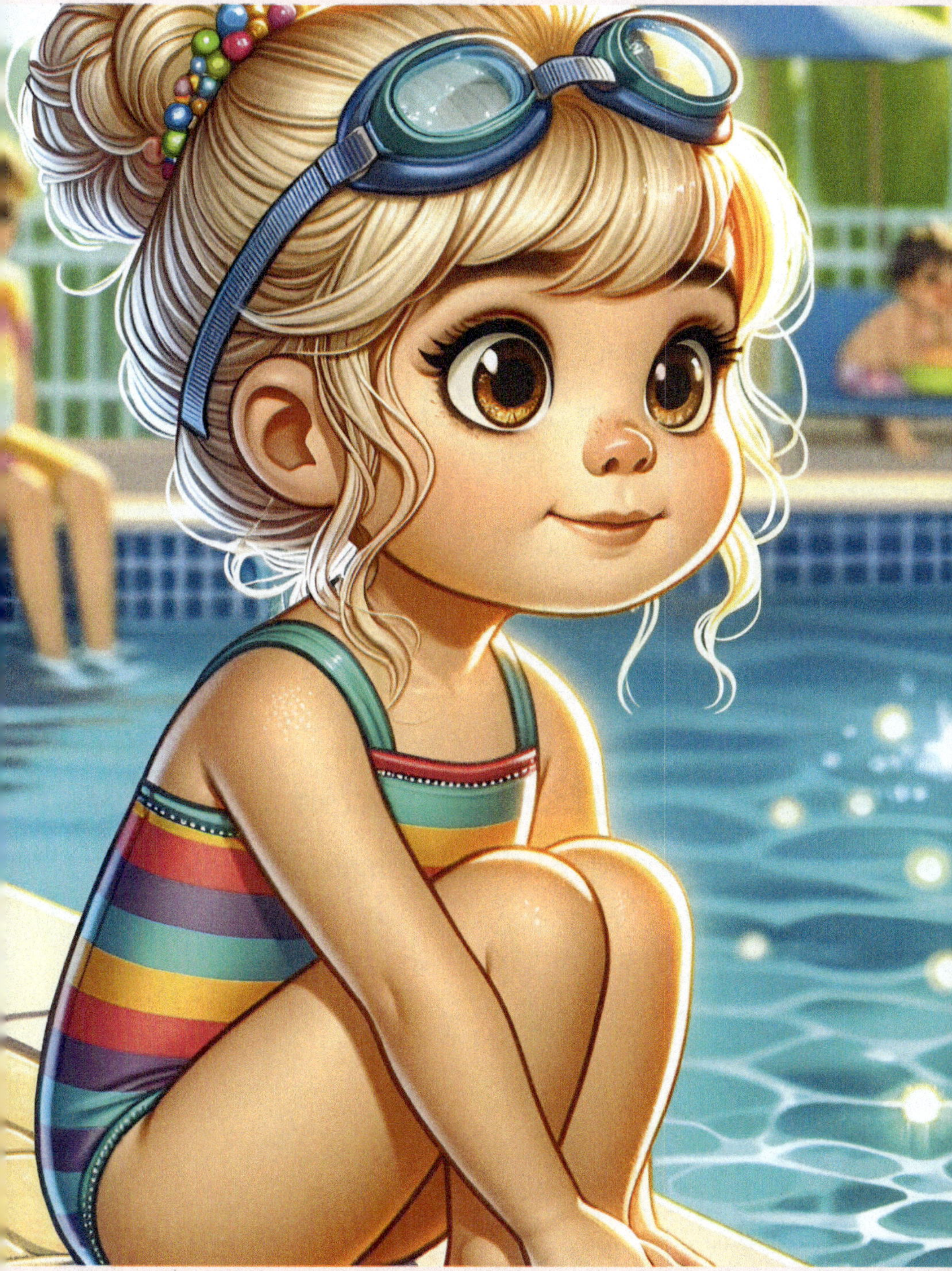

However, life was about to present Val with a new challenge that would test her resilience, her strength, but also her constant smile and joy.

The news that she would need surgery to install a metal device in her left leg to help it grow filled her with fear and anxiety.

Val knew she would face difficult times ahead, but she also knew she wouldn't be alone on her journey.

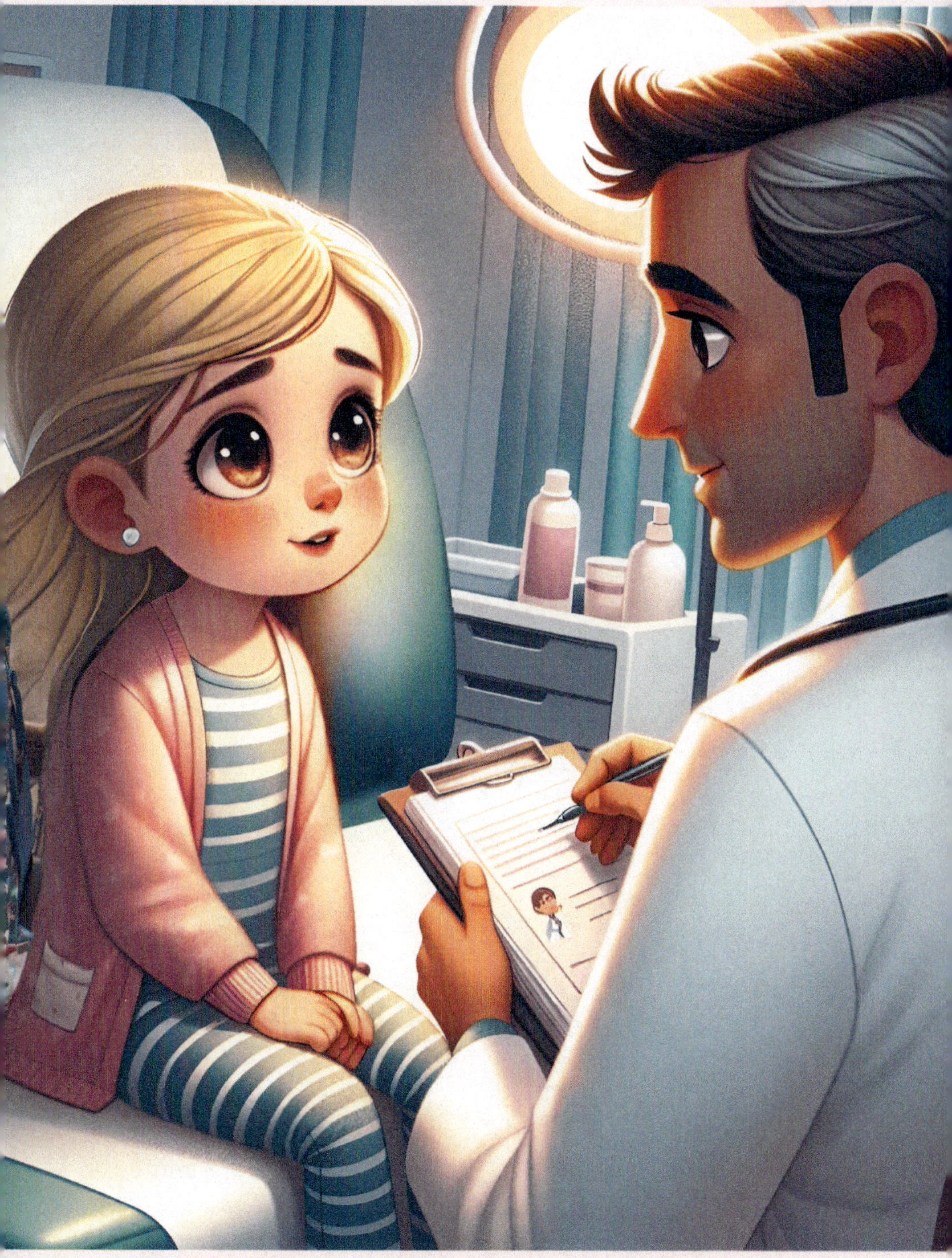

COURAGE

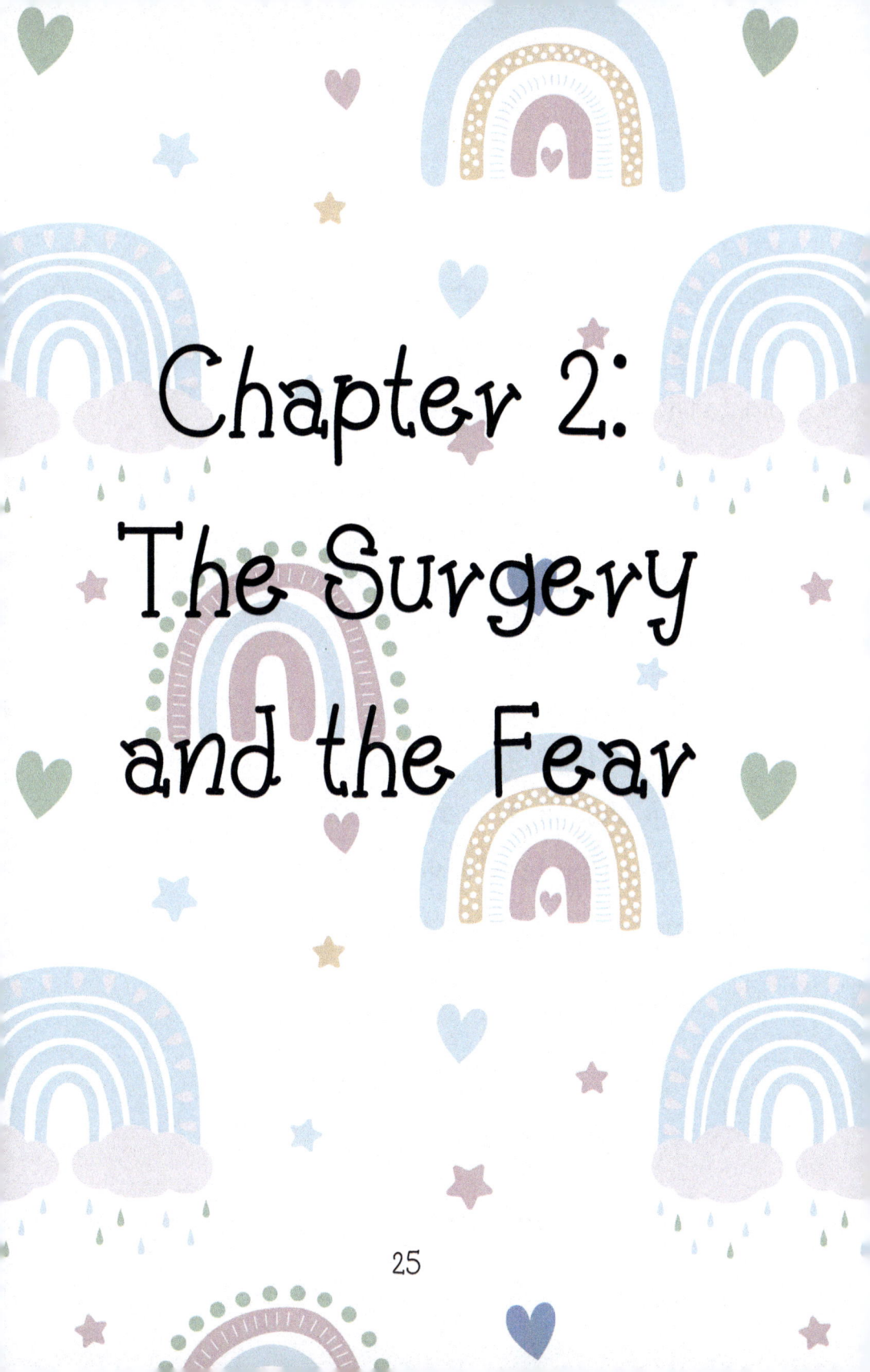

Chapter 2: The Surgery and the Fear

The thought of the upcoming surgery hung over Val like a dark cloud, filling her days with anxiety and her nights with restless dreams.

Even with the unwavering support of her family and the doctors' reassurances, Val couldn't help but feel nervous.

The idea of having a metal device in her leg was unsettling and frightening. "What if something goes wrong?" she worried. "What if I can't walk or swim like I used to?"

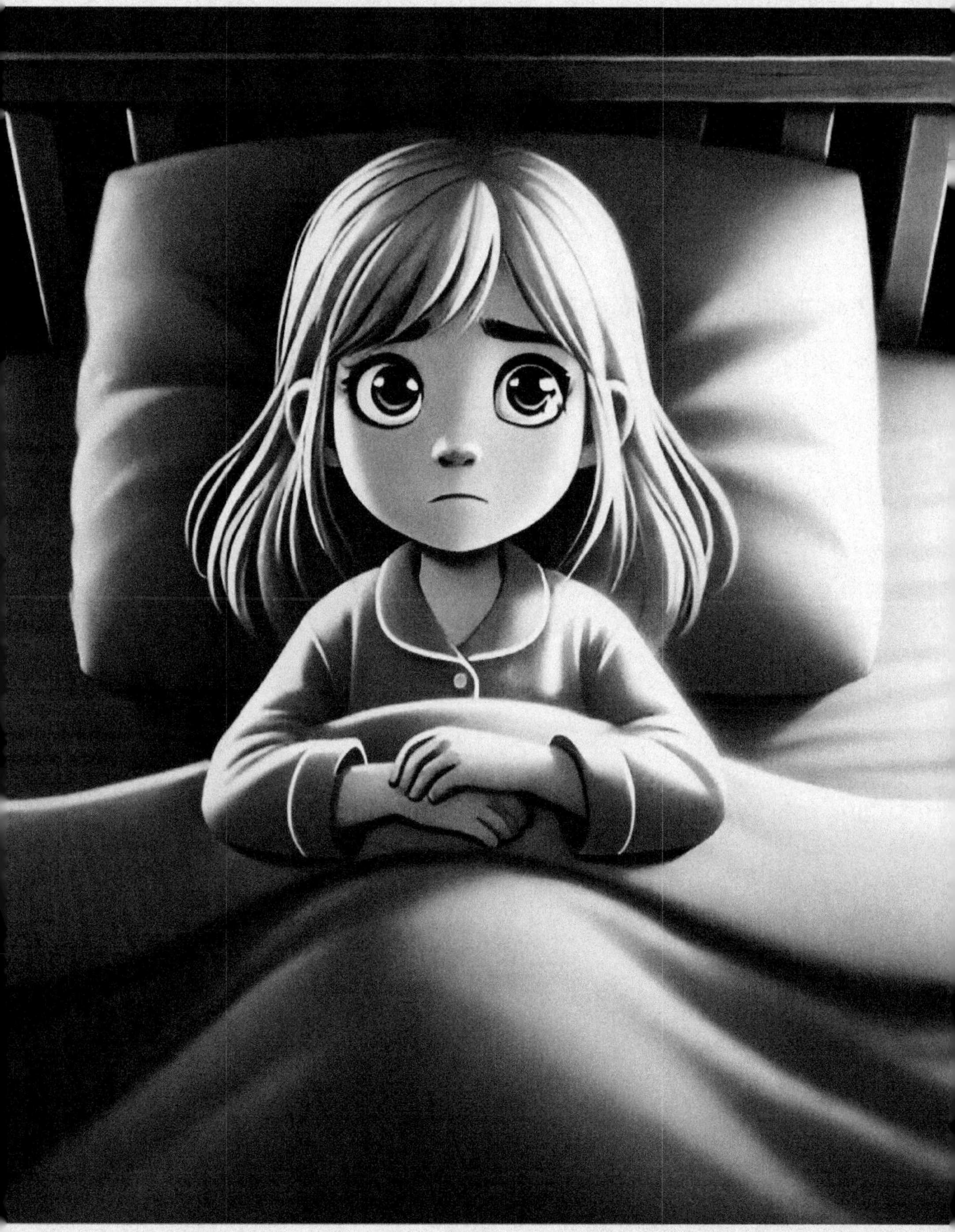

The day of the surgery arrived faster than Val had wanted.

After giving her parents a big hug, she was wheeled into the operating room.

As the anesthesia began to take effect, Val closed her eyes, trying to hold on to the image of herself swimming freely in the pool, her happy place.

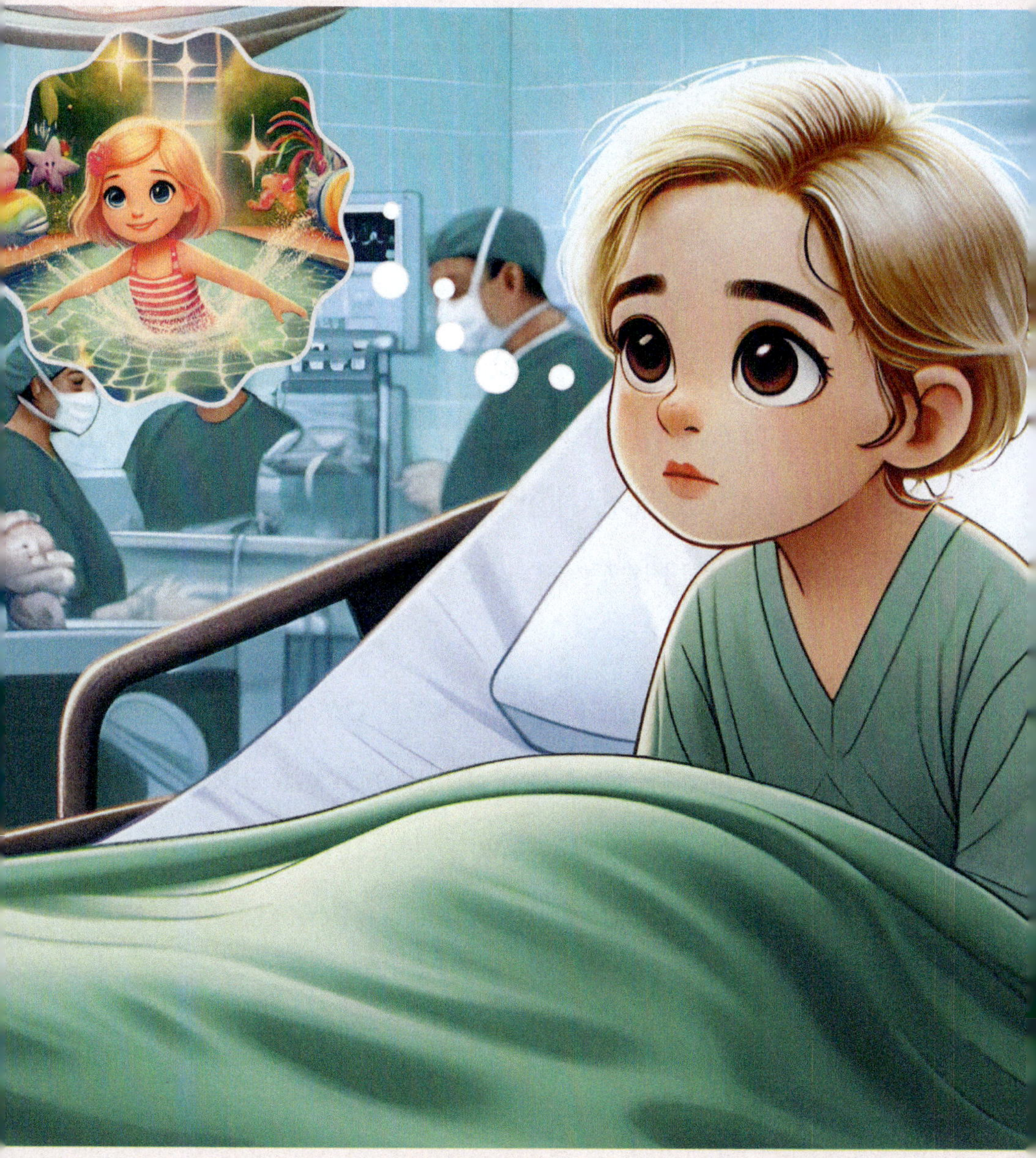

The surgery was successful, but the road to recovery was harder than Val had imagined.

The days in the hospital blurred together, life in a wheelchair was entirely new to her, and although she had the support of her family and the doctors who regularly visited her, filling her with encouragement and love, she couldn't help but feel different.

The presence of the large scar on her leg was a constant reminder of her condition, and although she knew it was a step towards improvement, the psychological downturn was visible.

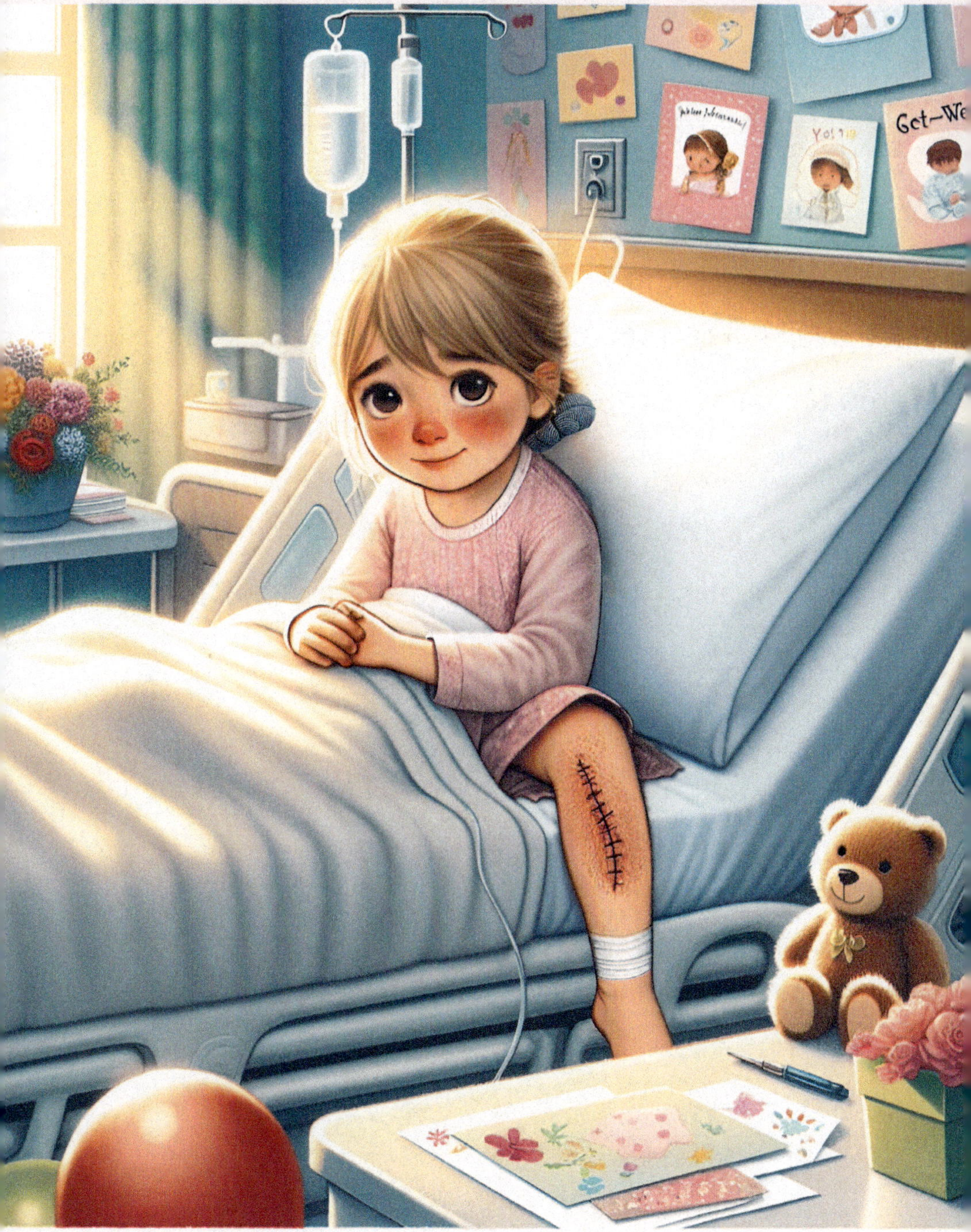

Val struggled to find the motivation to start physical therapy. The fear of feeling pain or not being able to do things as before paralyzed her.

However, her doctor, a patient and understanding woman, talked to her about the importance of taking small steps.

"Every day, a little stronger, a little closer to where you want to be," she would say.

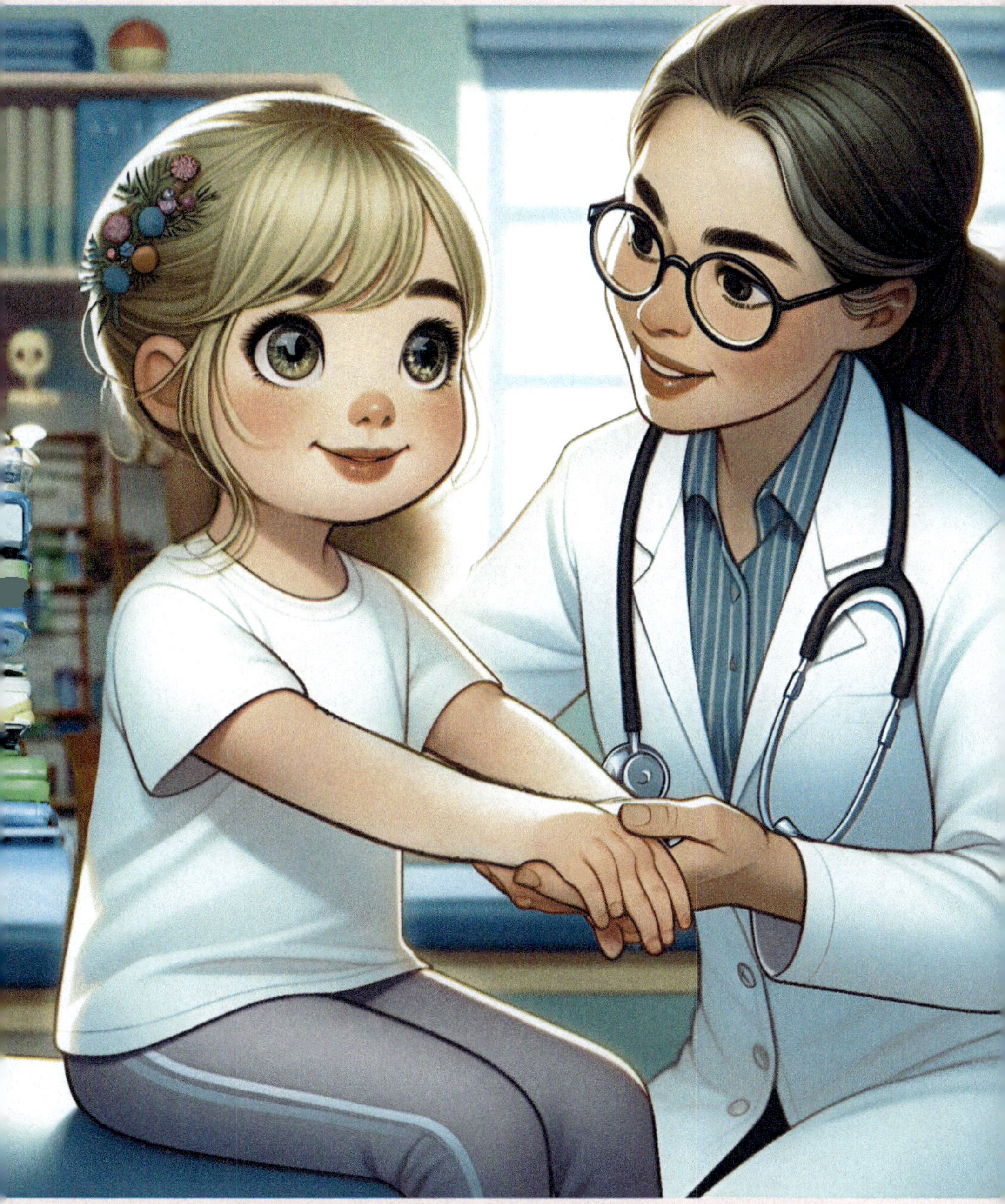

In those moments of doubt, every night before going to sleep, Val's mother started telling her stories of great women, full of courage and strength, who had overcome great adversities.

The first of these stories was about Sudha Chandran.

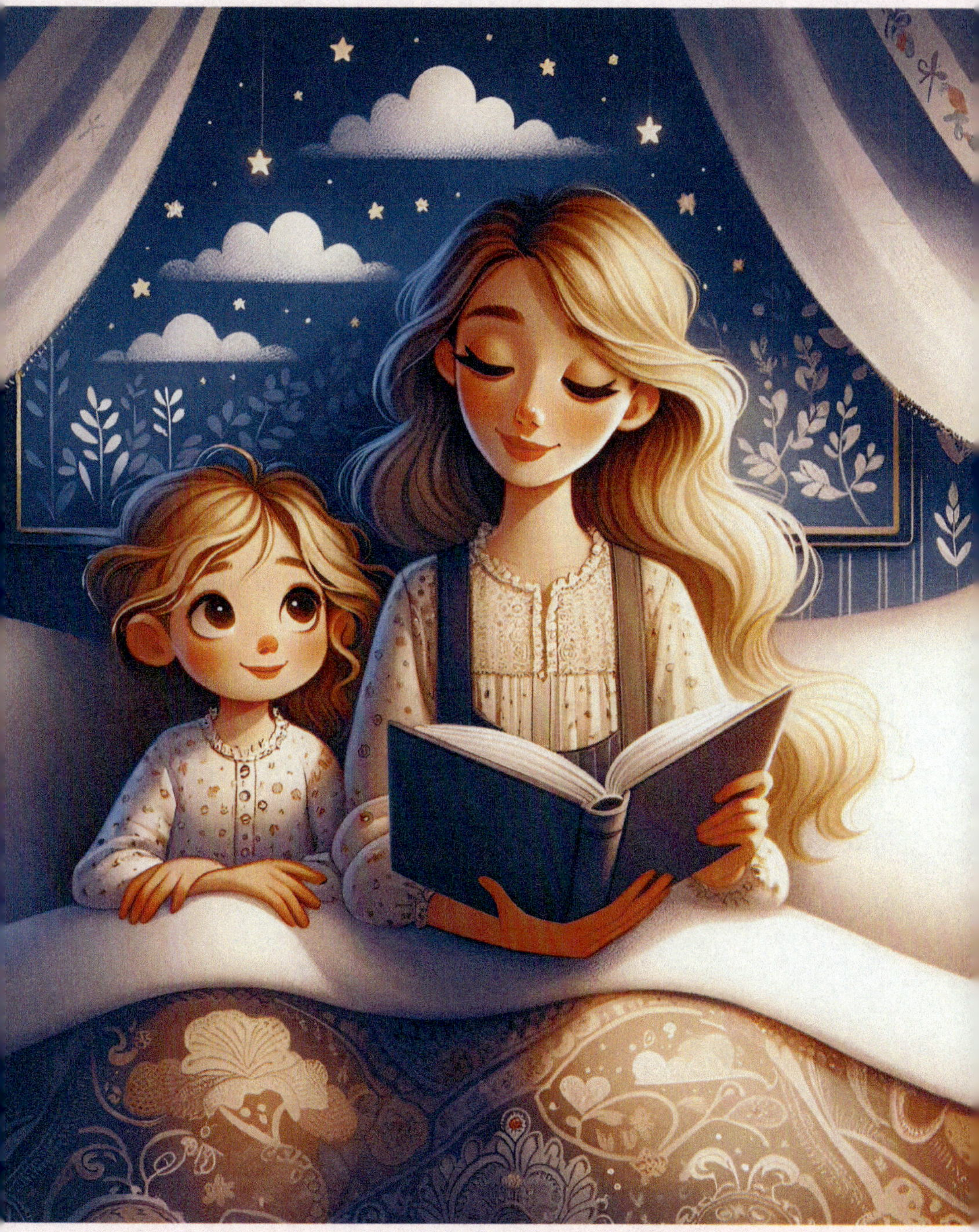

Sudha was a girl from India who, after losing a leg at the age of 16 due to a traffic accident and subsequent gangrene, did not give up. With the help of a prosthesis and firm determination, she decided not to be left behind, continuing her career as a dancer and becoming a global icon, inspiring others with her famous phrase "You don't need legs to dance."

Her relentless struggle and use of orthopedics allowed her to achieve her dreams against all odds. "If she could find a way to keep dancing, you will find a way to move forward too," her mother would say.

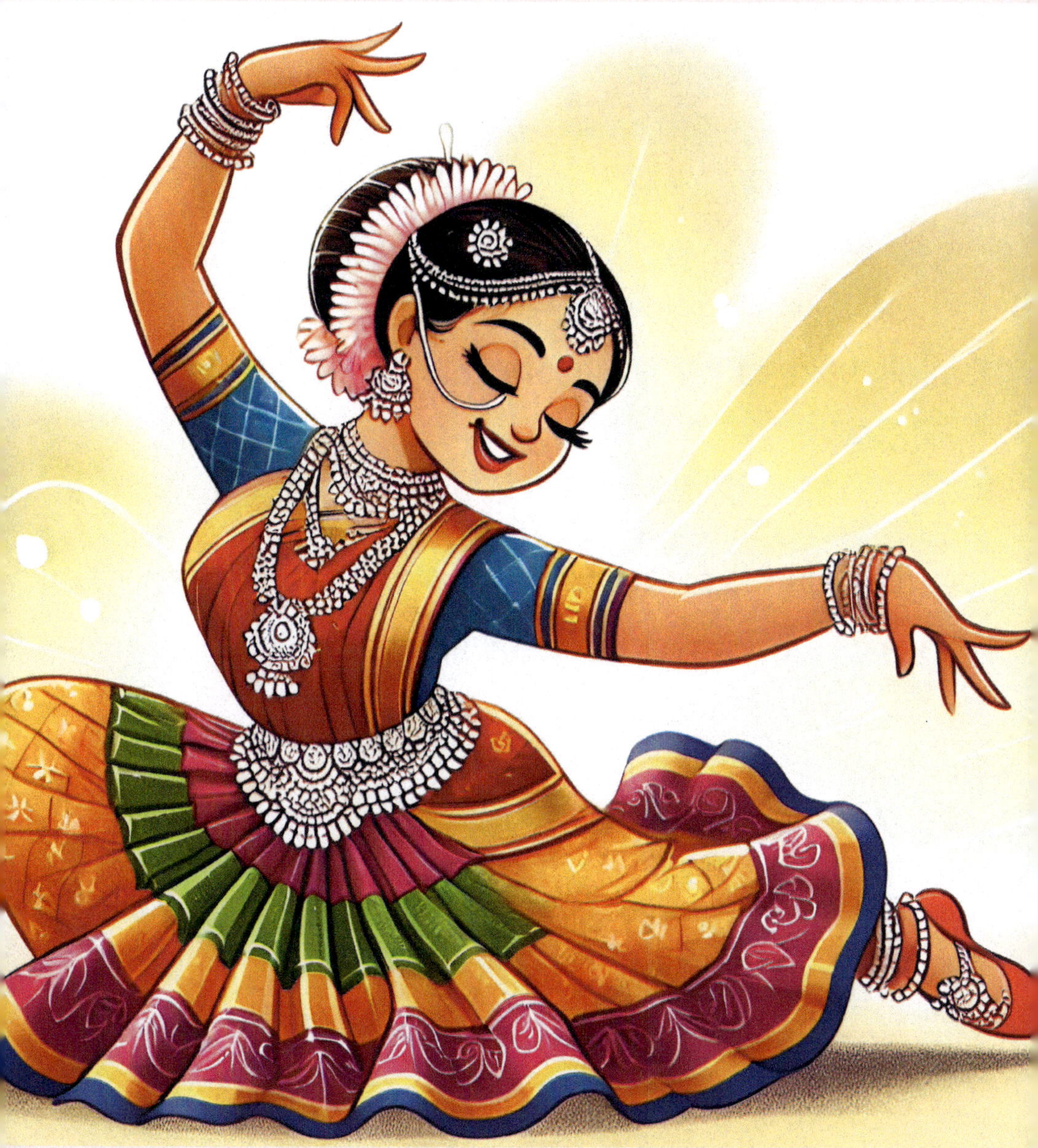

The next night, her mom told her another of those stories.

This time the protagonist was Jessica Cox. She was an example of overcoming and limitless ability.

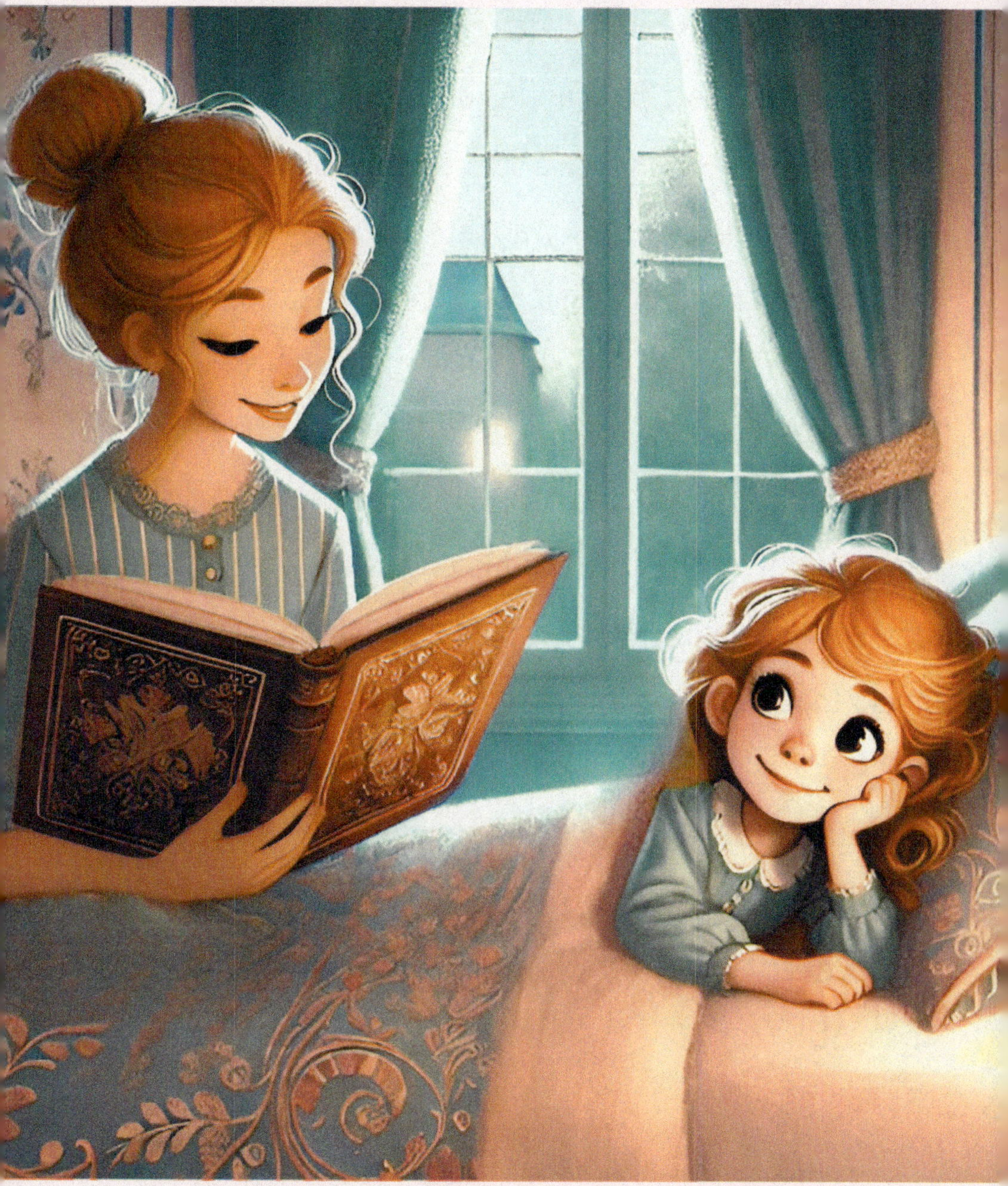

Born without arms, she became the first person to earn a black belt in martial arts and a pilot's license, achieving a Guinness World Record. She also became a certified diver and graduated in psychology from the University of Arizona. She visited over 26 countries, sharing her inspiring message and founded Rightfooted Foundation International to support children with disabilities. Jessica never let her disability stop her from achieving her dreams. Living a normal life, using her feet as her hands, she reached goals that other people can only dream of.

Jessica's determination and her message of never giving up deeply resonated with Val. "If she could achieve so many goals, I can do anything too," she thought.

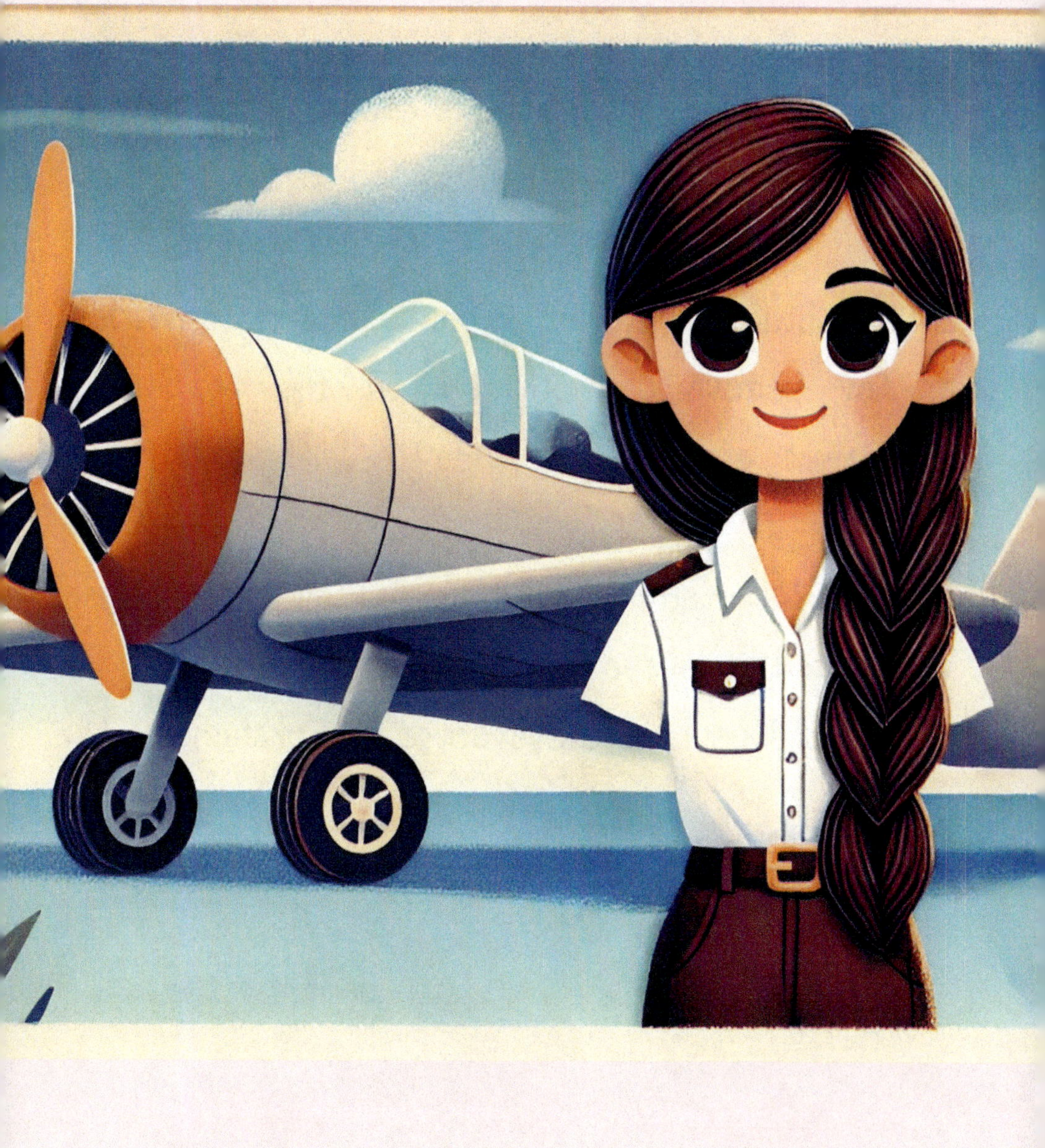

These stories began to plant a seed of hope in Val's heart.

Little by little, she started to participate more actively in her recovery, motivated by the stories of overcoming she heard every day.

Although the road was still long and full of challenges, Val started to believe that, just like the heroines in the stories, she could also overcome any obstacle in her way.

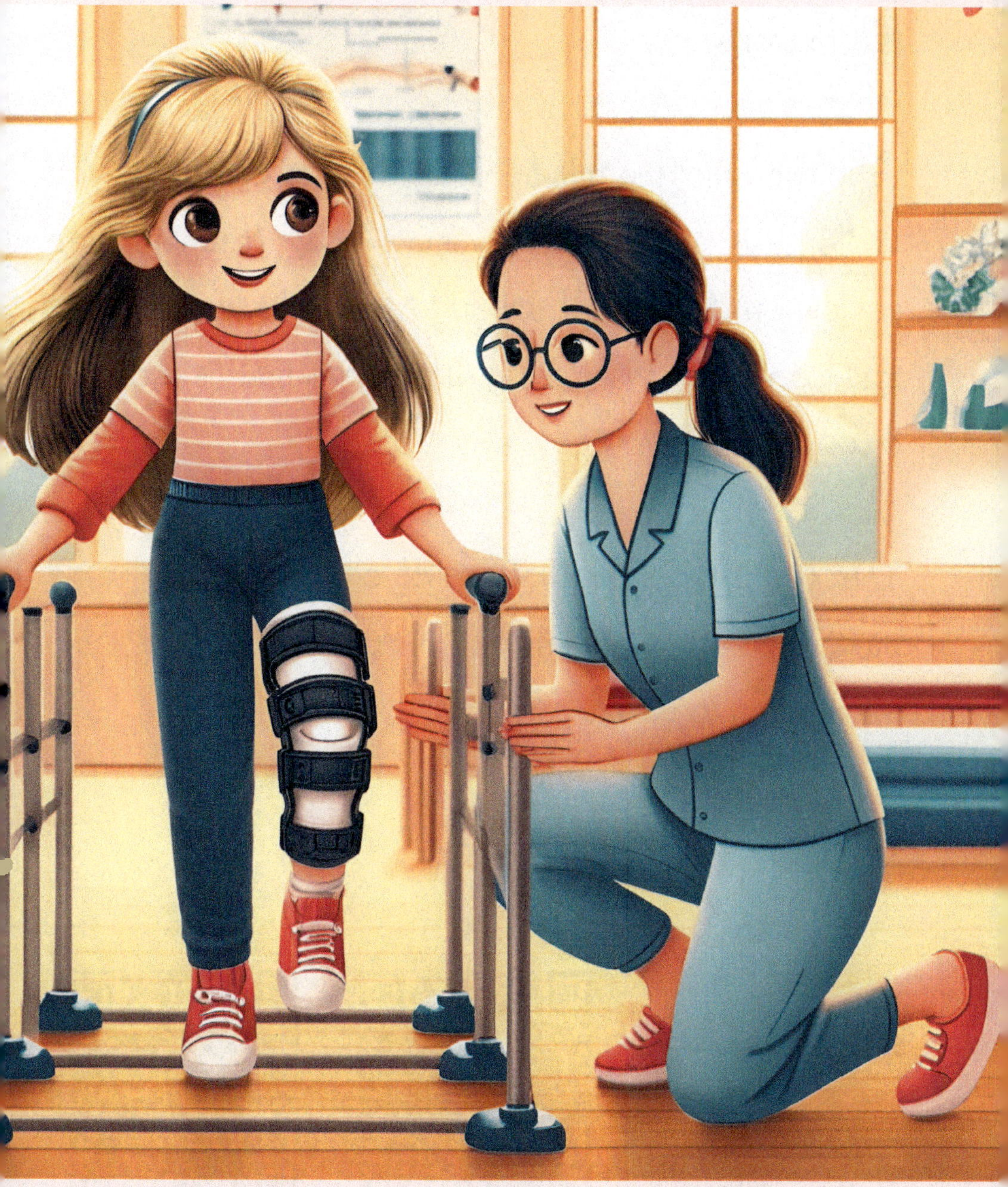

Your opinion is truly unique, and it means so much to us and to others who might be searching for a story like this one.

If you're enjoying this book, we'd be so grateful if you could take a moment to share your thoughts in a review on Amazon. It doesn't have to be long—just a few words can make a big difference and help others discover this story.

Thank you from the bottom of our hearts for being part of this adventure. Your support means everything to us. ●

With love,

US

UK

Grow Positive Thoughts

Never Stop Dreaming

you're AMAZING as you are

You are strong

Smile

Be TRUE to YOURSELF

CONFIDENCE

Chapter 3: Inspiration and First Steps

As Val recovered, her room at home filled up with books and stories about girls and women who had overcome incredible challenges.

Each story was a thread of hope, teaching her that no matter how big the obstacle, it could be overcome with determination and support.

Among the pages of these stories, Val found not only inspiration but also an invisible community of fighters who, unknowingly, were helping her rise.

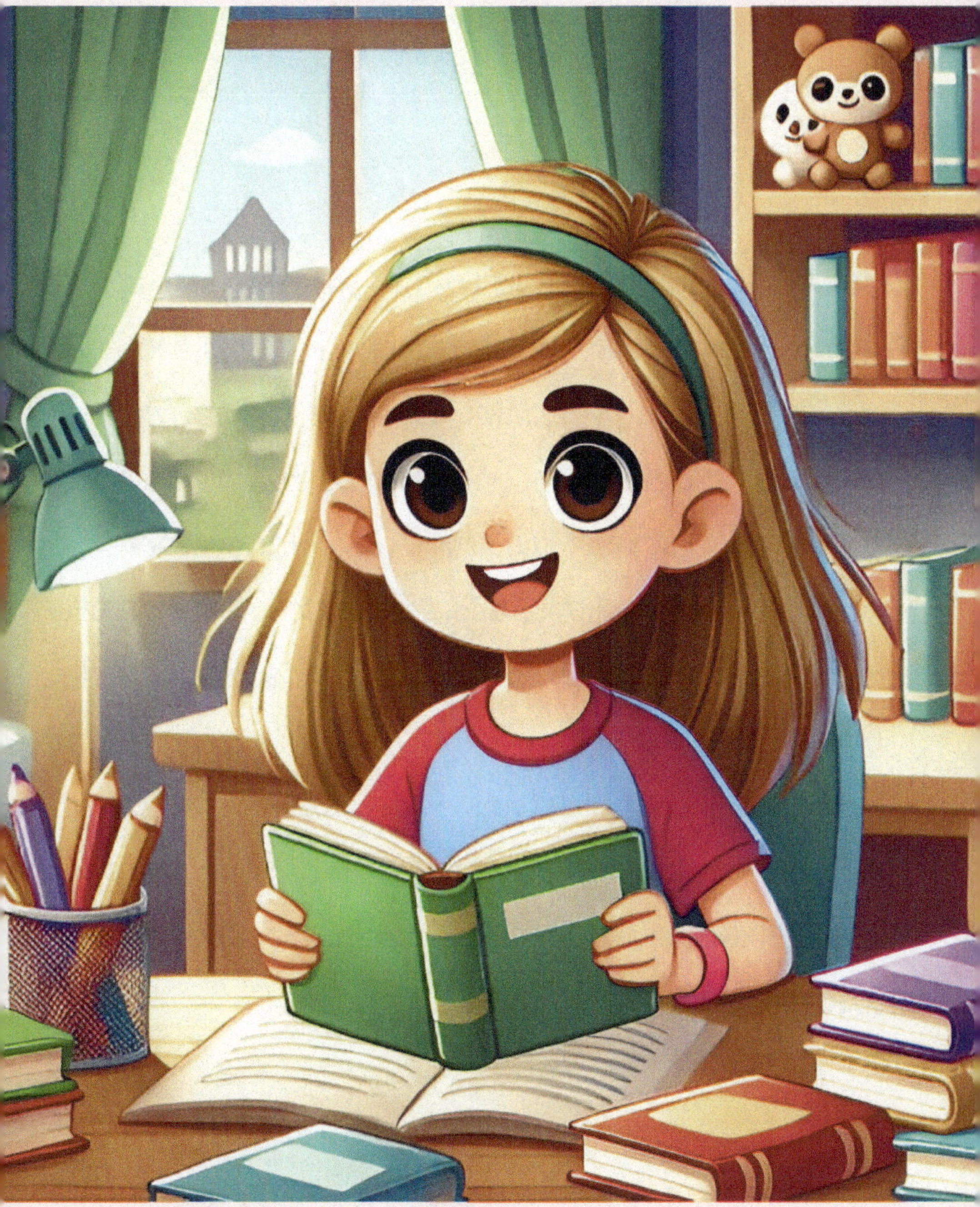

One of the stories that touched her the most was that of Helen Keller.

Helen was an American writer, speaker, and activist who had been blind and deaf since she was two years old, becoming a prominent advocate for the rights of people with disabilities. She created her own alphabet at age 7, became the first deaf-blind woman to graduate from college, and championed humanitarian causes and workers' rights. She founded Helen Keller International, visited over 35 countries, and wrote inspiring books about her life and philosophy of inclusion. Helen used to say: "The best and most beautiful things in the world cannot be seen or even touched, they must be felt with the heart."

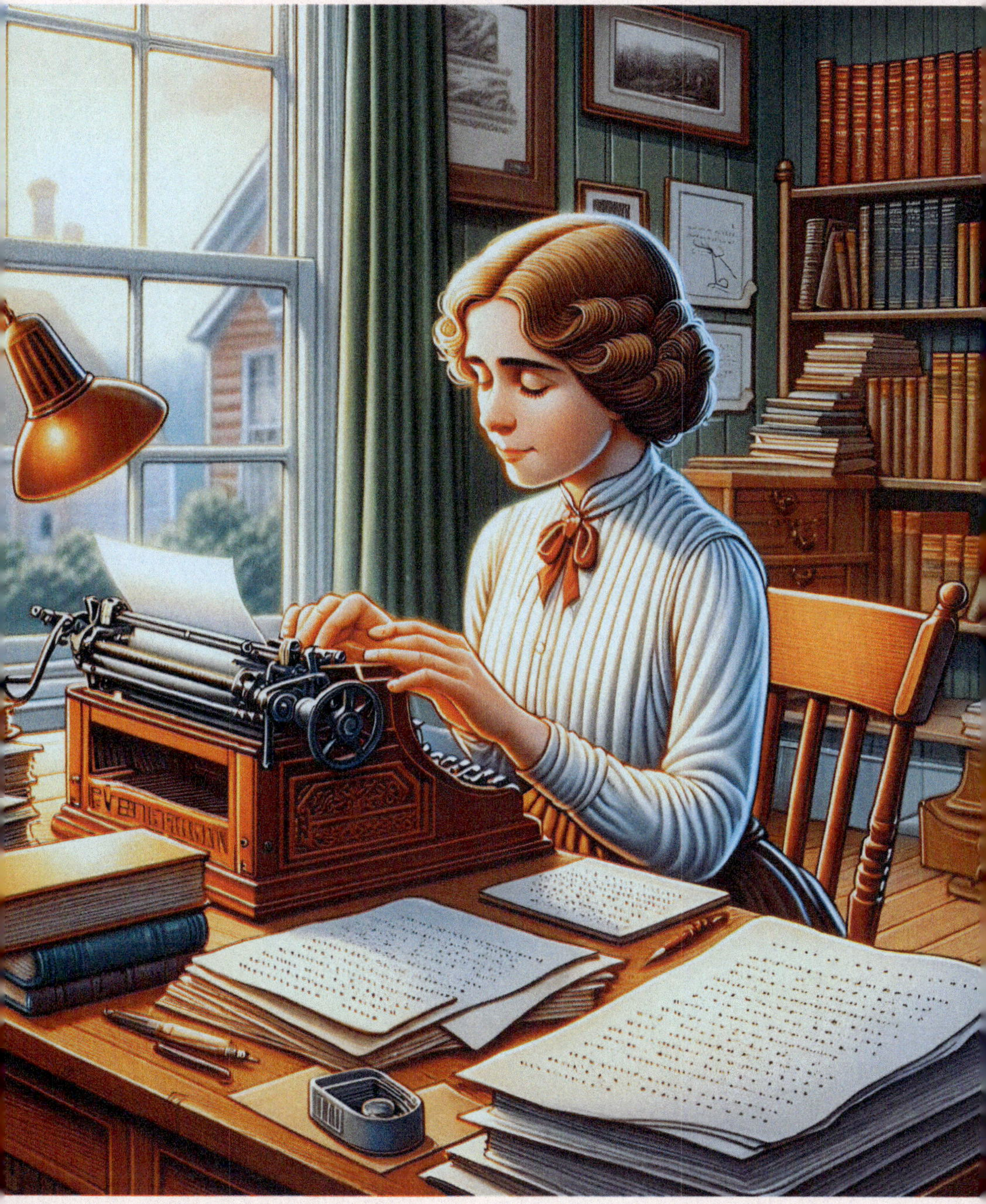

Val felt very inspired by this story, and with this new mindset, she started facing physical therapy with a different attitude.

Every exercise, every step taken, was a triumph, a celebration.

Although there were tough days, the image of Sudha Chandran, Jessica Cox, Helen Keller, and many others pushed her to keep going.

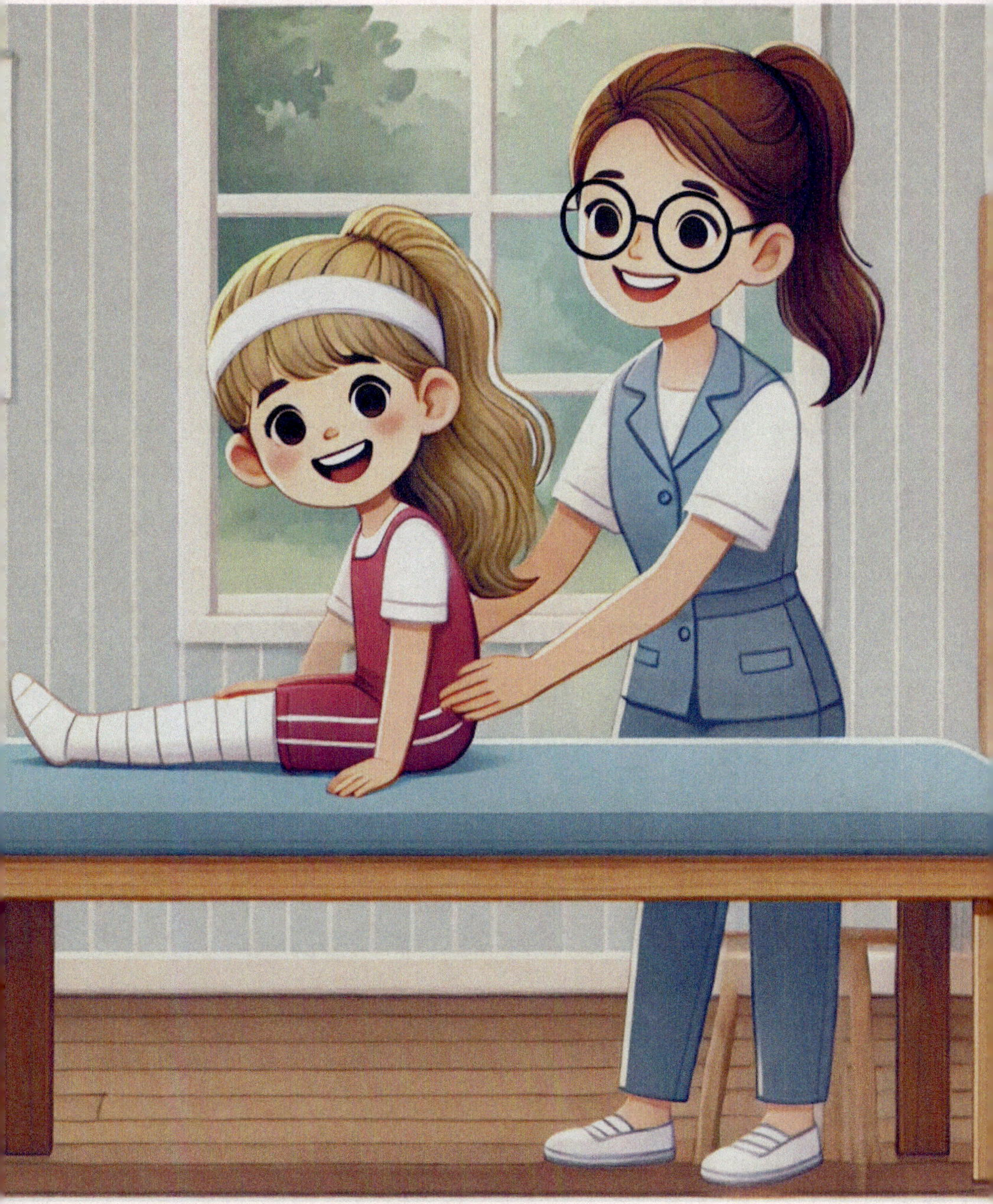

Val began sharing her own fears and achievements with her physical therapist, opening up more and allowing herself to be vulnerable.

This act of sharing not only relieved her but also strengthened her resilience.

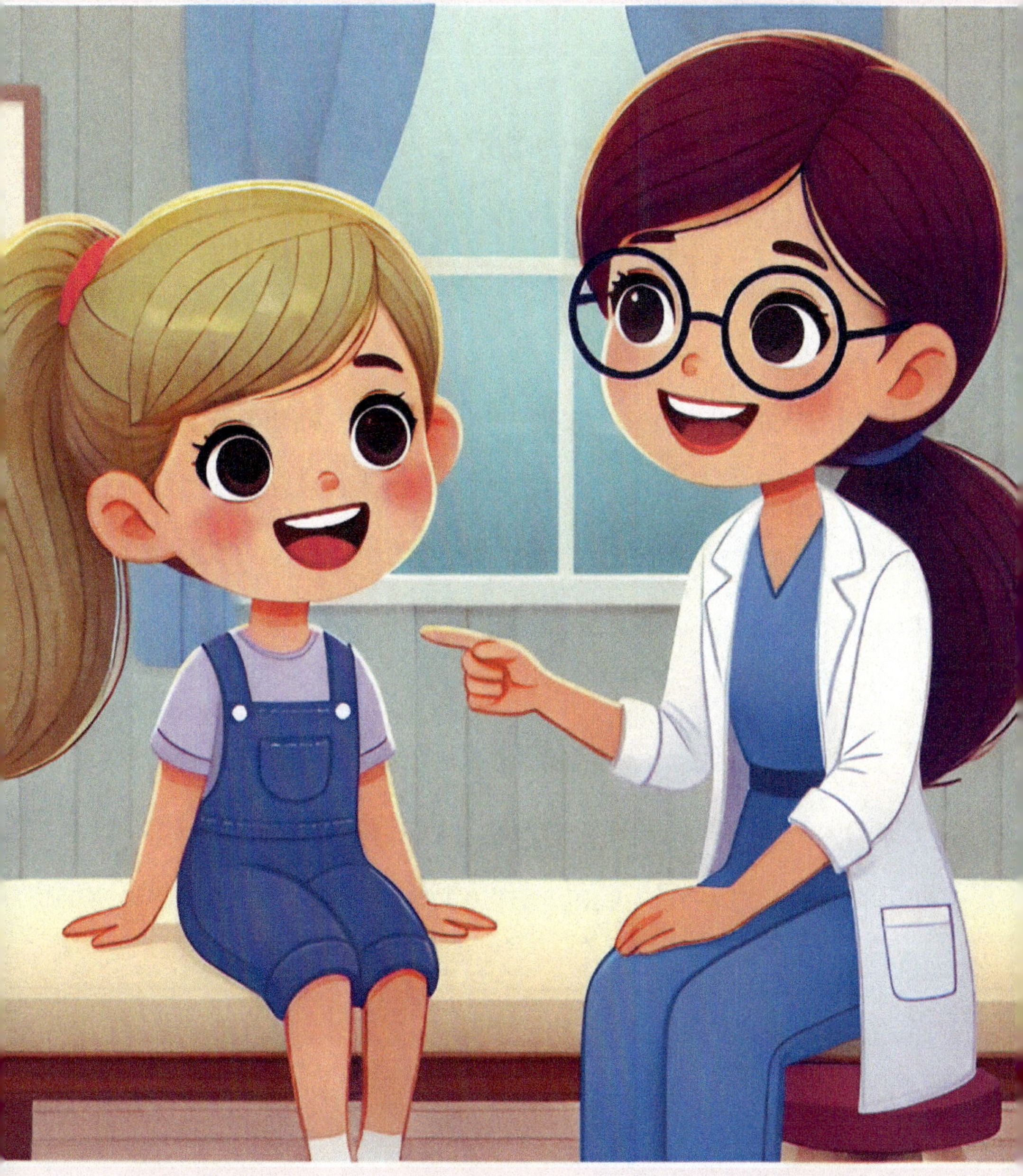

Friendship played a crucial role in her recovery. Her school friends visited her regularly, bringing her drawings and letters of encouragement.

They even pushed her wheelchair while they talked and laughed, telling anecdotes and talking about future plans. Val realized that, although her journey was personal, she was not alone.

The community around her — her family, friends, and even people she only knew through stories — formed a support network that enveloped her with love and strength.

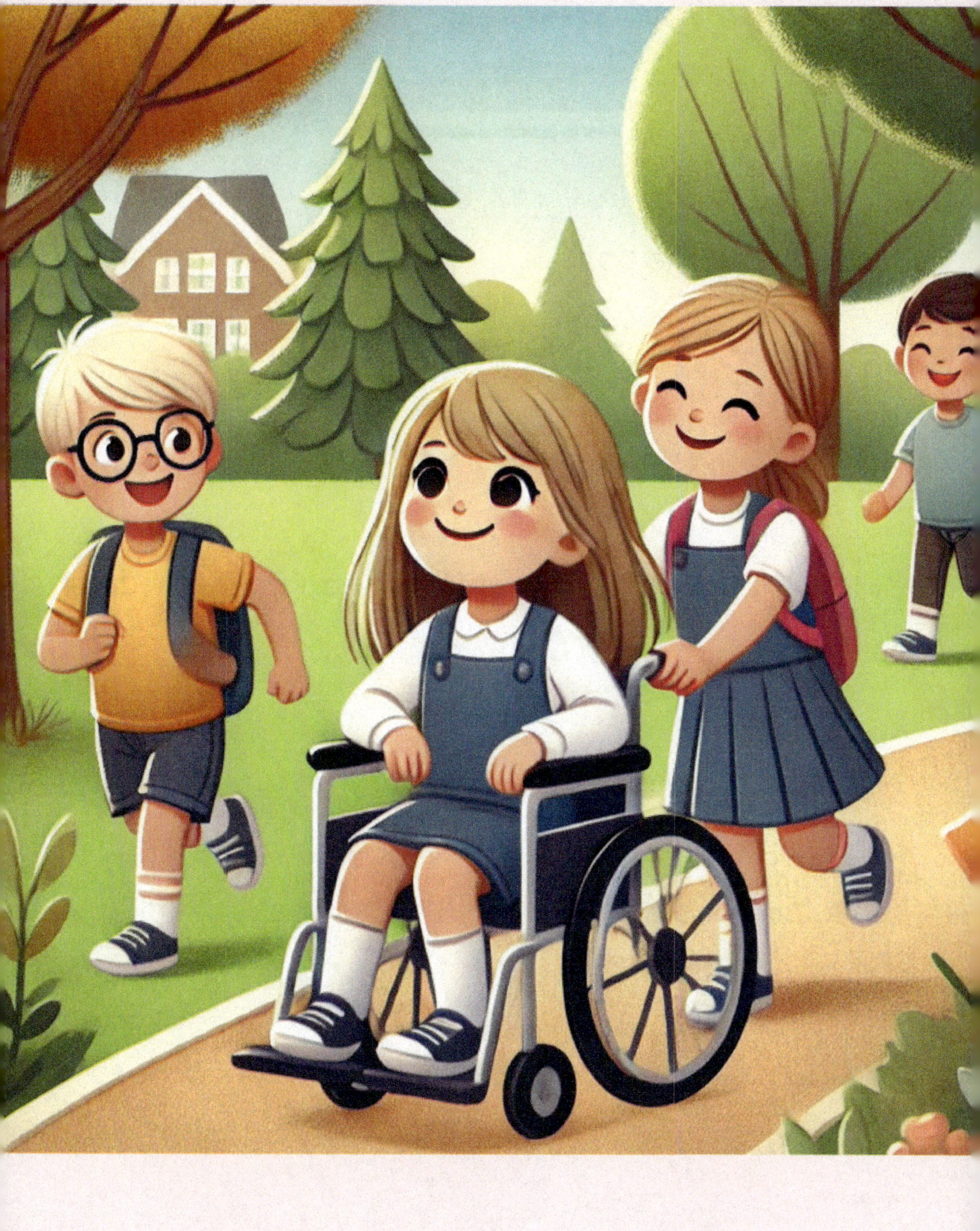

One day, determined to resume her passion, Val asked to visit the pool.

Although at first, she felt insecure, the water returned a sense of normalcy and freedom to her.

Swimming once again became her refuge, her place of power.

With each stroke, Val felt her confidence grow. "I'm becoming myself again," she thought with a smile that reflected not only happiness but also deep gratitude.

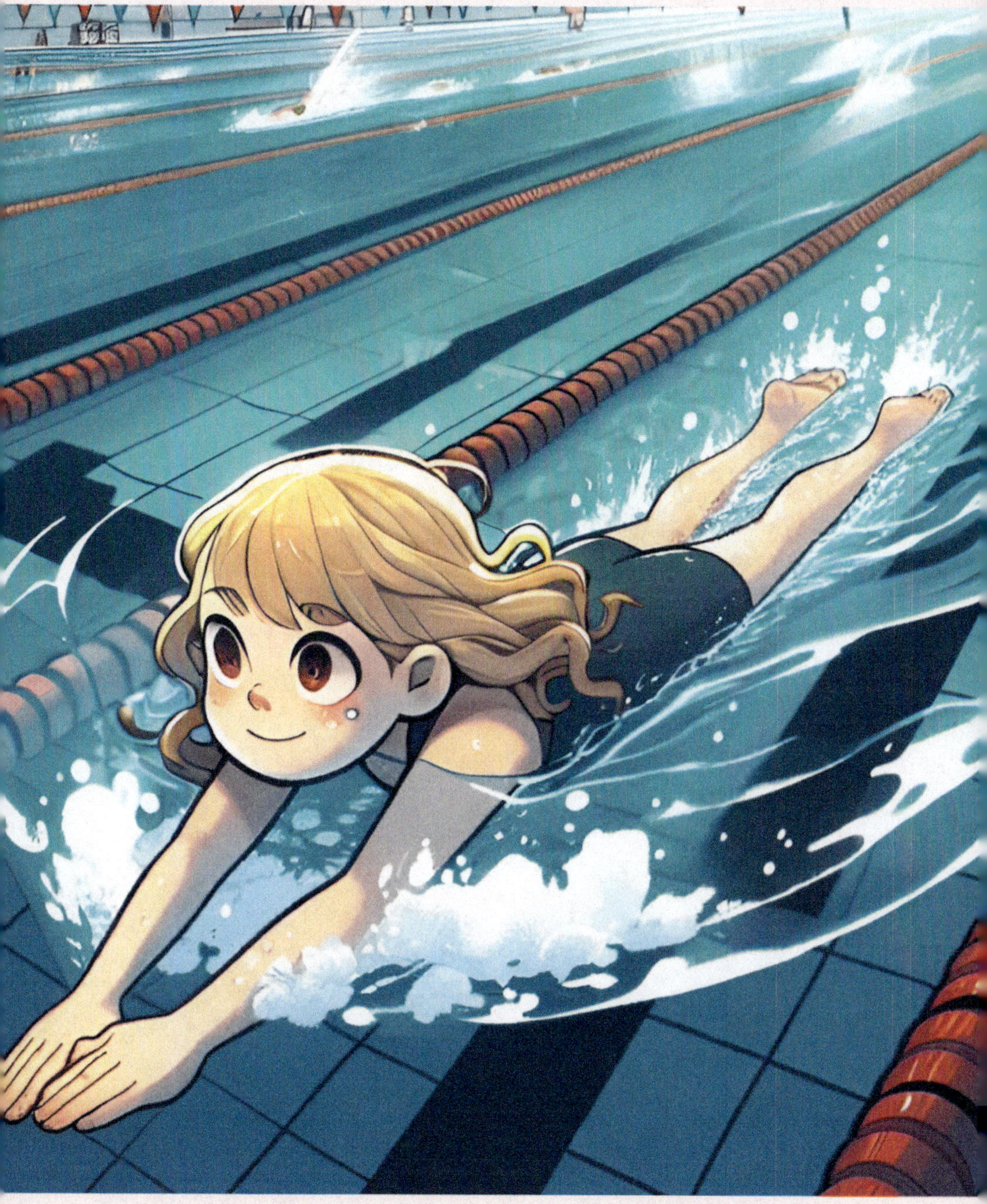

HOPE

Chapter 4: Overcoming and New Horizons

As the months went by, Val made progress and overcame challenges.

She gradually started walking with the help of crutches and continued swimming, not just to strengthen her muscles but for the sense of freedom she felt in the water.

She was no longer just the girl who had undergone surgery and faced the uncertainty of recovery; she was a swimmer with a powerful story of triumph, inspiring everyone who knew her journey.

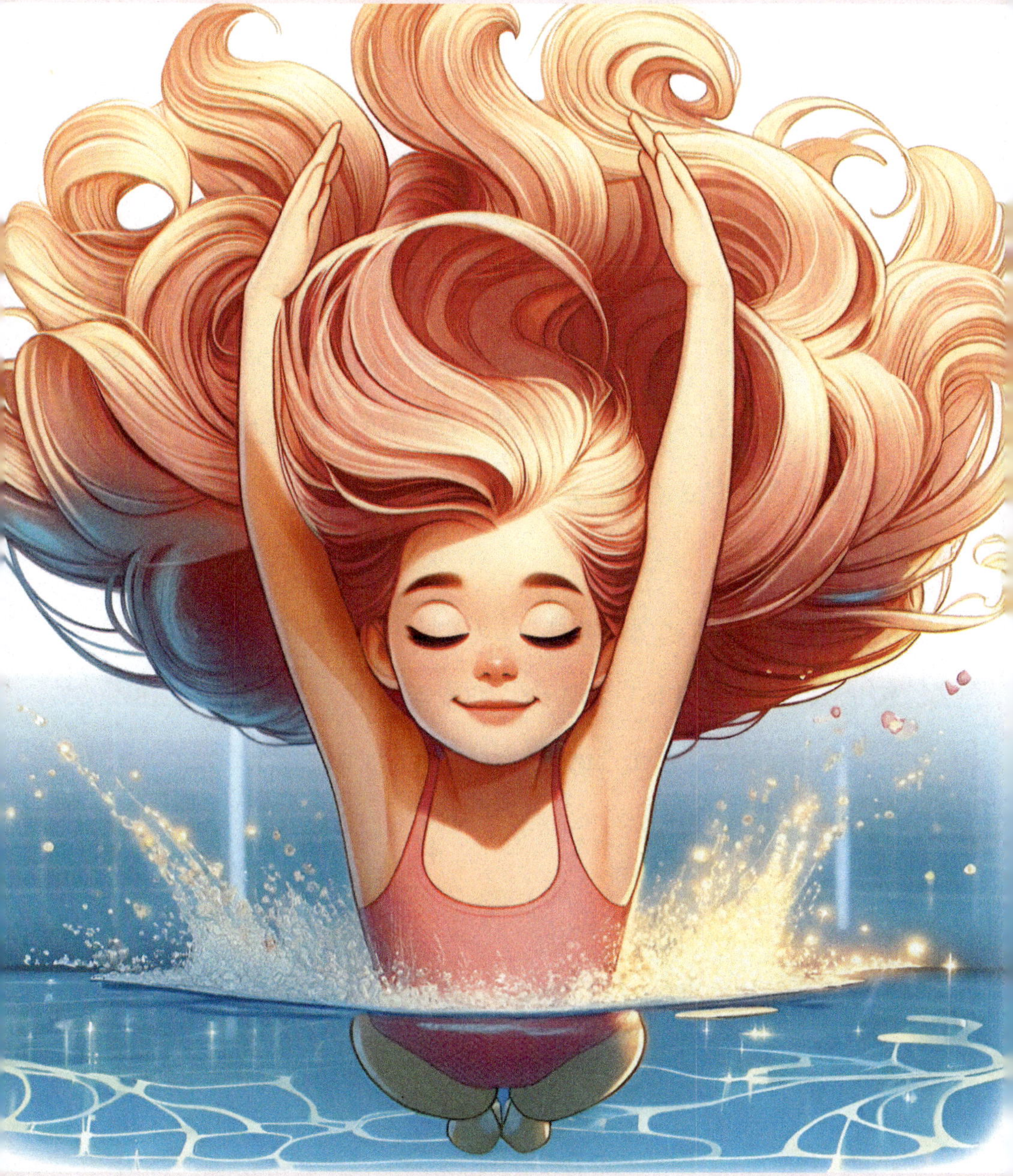

Time went on, and Val kept achieving more goals, thanks to her hard work, her determination to overcome, and the unwavering support of her family and friends. She felt herself growing on the inside, and it showed on the outside.

She felt accomplished, happy, strong, loved, and motivated to achieve even more. This motivated her to set her next big goal: to compete in swimming competitions.

65

The first time Val competed after her surgery, the atmosphere was thick with tension and excitement.

Standing on the starting block, she felt a whirlwind of emotions: fear, pride, nervousness, but most of all, immense gratitude for having come this far.

At that moment, she remembered another story her mom had told her one night before bed.

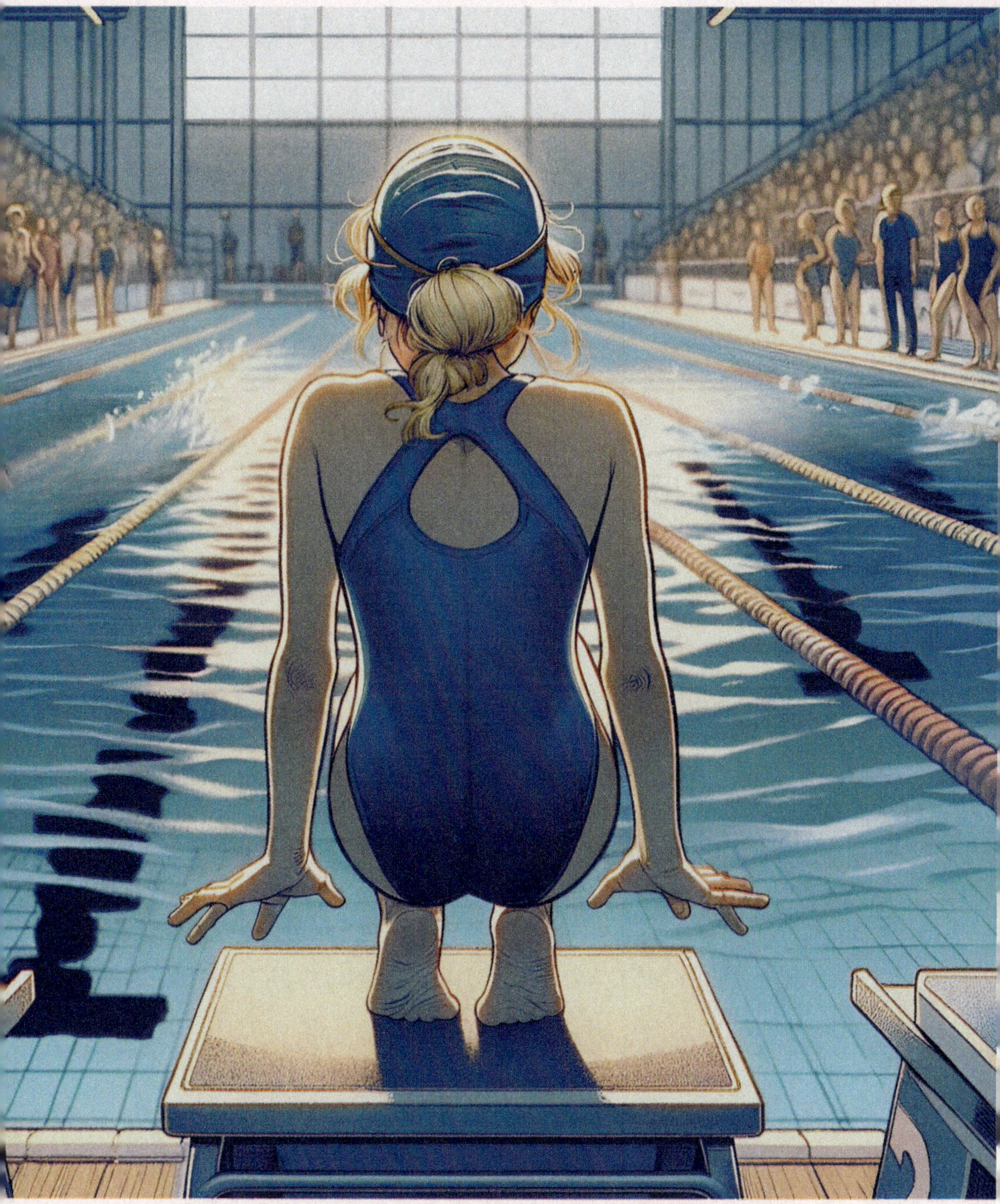

The story of Amy Purdy, who lost her legs, spleen, and hearing in one ear due to an illness. Despite this, she became an elite athlete, best-selling author, and motivational speaker.

She quickly adapted to using prosthetics and became a Paralympic medalist. She overcame numerous challenges, including multiple surgeries, and promoted gratitude and taking life one step at a time to face adversities. She also had to go through changes like adjusting new prostheses for her legs, making her an inspiration. Her saying: 'We must take things day by day, making progress little by little. It's important to look for what we are grateful for in life and remember that each day brings new light and new opportunities" really resonated with Val.

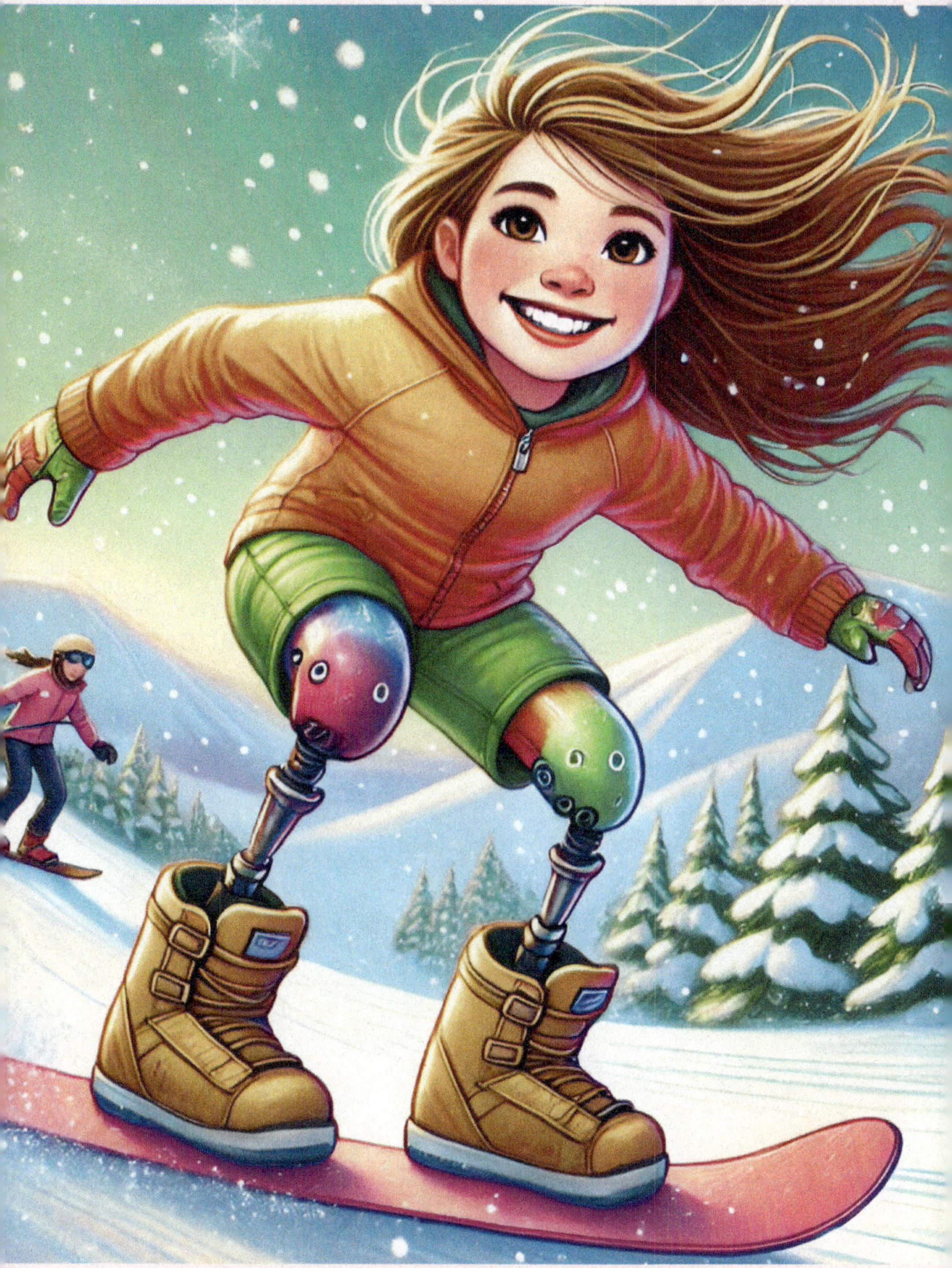

As she dove into the water, all those emotions transformed into energy, propelling her through the pool.

It didn't matter if she won or lost; what mattered was that she was there, swimming and pushing her own limits.

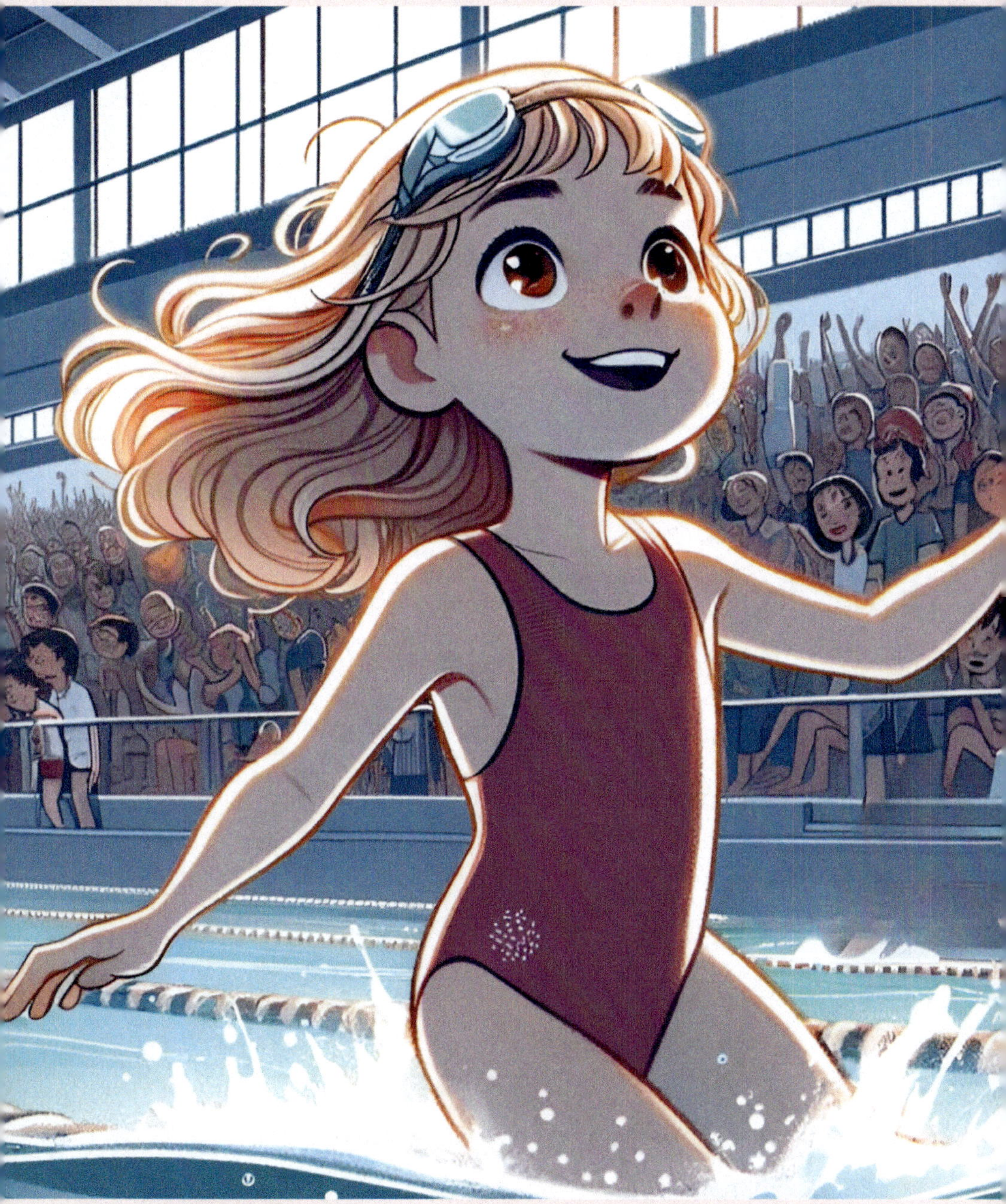

After the competition, Val was surrounded by friends, family, and teammates, all celebrating not only her return to swimming but also the journey she had undertaken to reach that moment.

It was then that Val realized her story wasn't just hers; it was also a testament to the strength of the human spirit, capable of overcoming obstacles and moving forward.

73

Inspired by this realization, Val decided to share her story with other girls facing their own challenges.

She began speaking at schools and hospitals, sharing her experiences and how the stories of others had given her hope and strength.

Val wanted to be like Jessica Cox, Sudha Chandran, and many others who had inspired her: a beacon of hope for others.

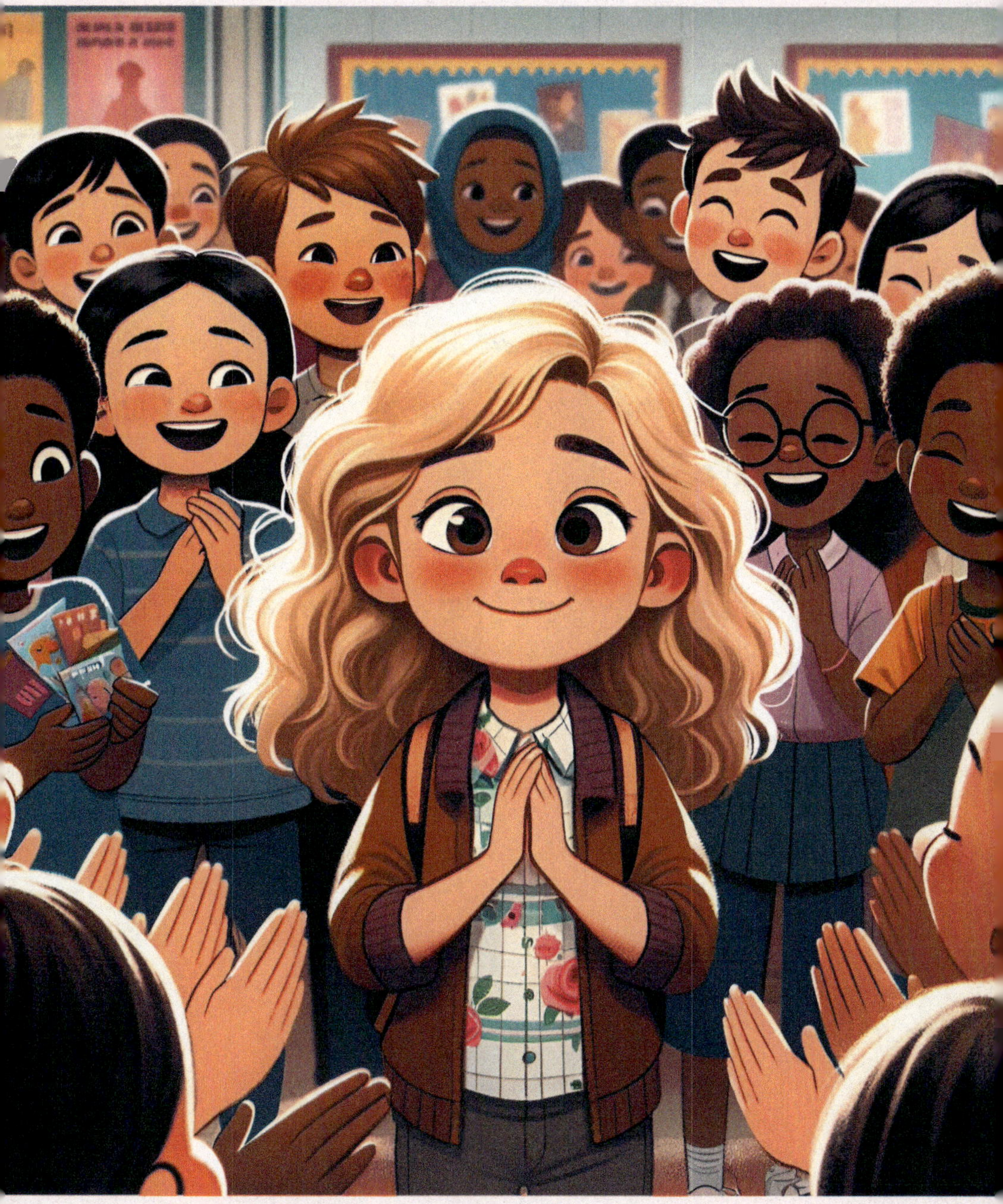

In each talk, Val emphasized the importance of friendship, self-confidence, and the courage to share and face fears.

She spoke about how each person can inspire others simply by facing challenges with determination, energy, and hope.

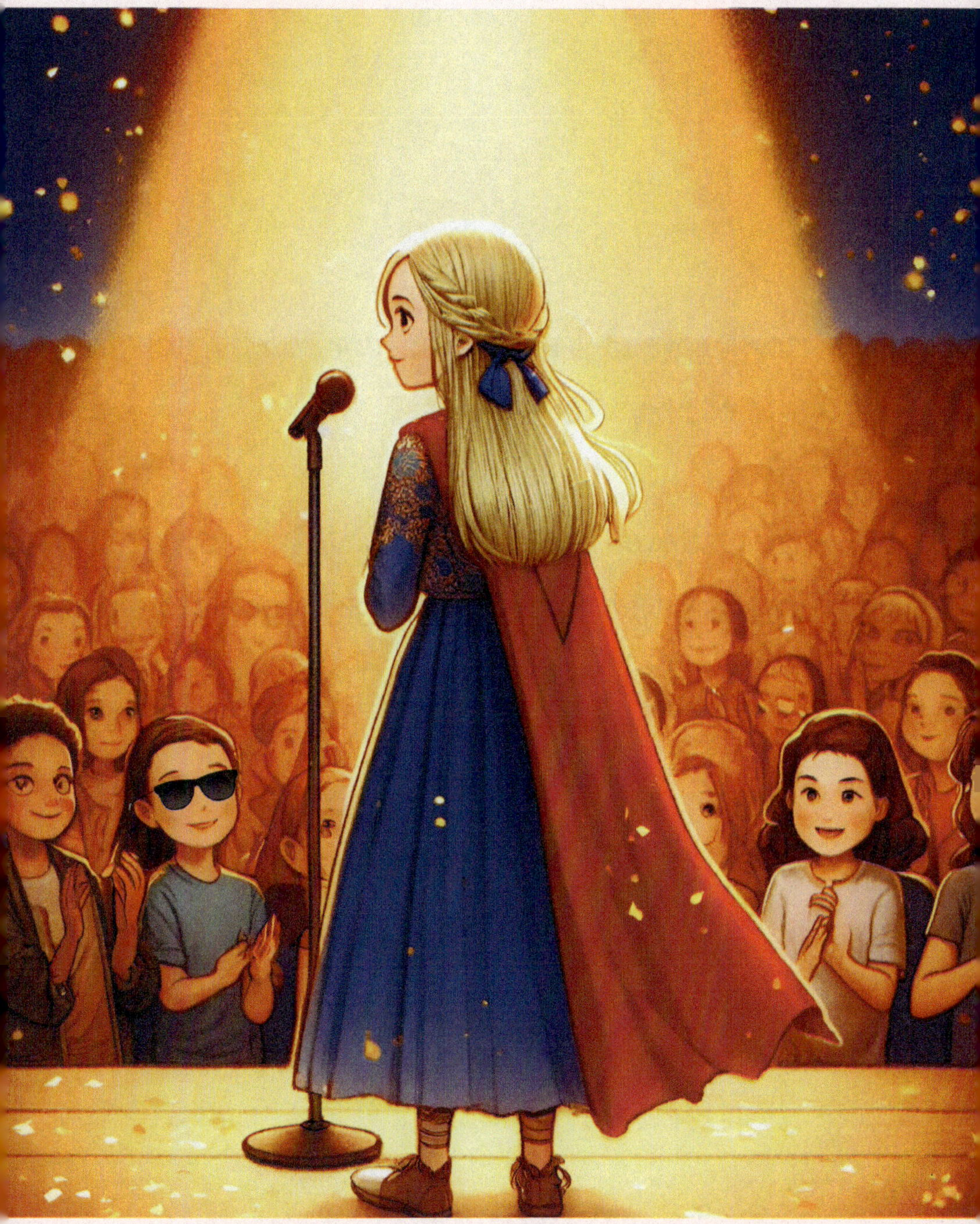

Val's story spread beyond her community, touching the hearts of people of all ages.

But what mattered most to her was knowing that, in some way, she was helping other girls feel less alone, more understood, and capable of facing their own challenges.

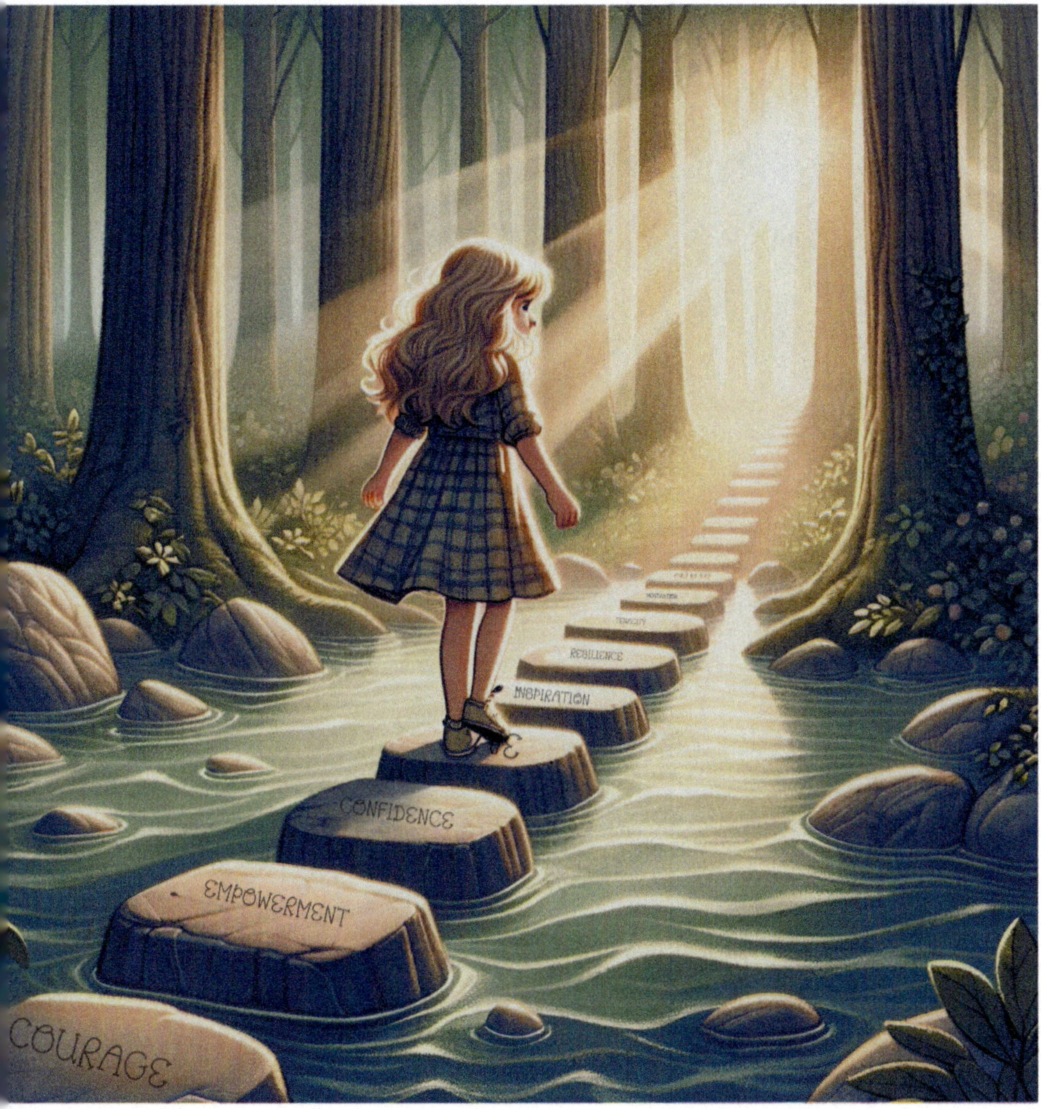
COURAGE
EMPOWERMENT
CONFIDENCE
INSPIRATION
RESILIENCE

Thank you, brave readers, for joining us on this exciting adventure! We hope that the story of our little heroine's triumph inspires you to believe in yourselves, fight for your dreams, and never give up. Always remember that you carry an incredible strength within you, capable of overcoming any obstacle.

We encourage you to face challenges with a smile and share this story with those around you.

The future is yours and full of possibilities! Never forget that you are the heroines of your own story.

Keep shining and conquering the world!

Printed in Great Britain
by Amazon